Scott Foresman
SCIENCE

Lab Manual Teacher's Edition

Grade 5

D1285898

Scott Foresman

Editorial Offices: Glenview, Illinois; Parsippany, New Jersey; New York, New York
Sales Offices: Reading, Massachusetts; Duluth, Georgia; Glenview, Illinois
Carrollton, Texas; Ontario, California

www.sfscience.com

Contributors

Series Authors

Dr. Timothy Cooney
*Professor of Earth Science and
  Science Education*
Earth Science Department
University of Northern Iowa
Cedar Falls, Iowa

Michael Anthony Dispezio
Science Education Specialist
Cape Cod Children's Museum
Falmouth, Massachusetts

Barbara K. Foots
Science Education Consultant
Houston, Texas

Dr. Angie L. Matamoros
Science Curriculum Specialist
Broward County Schools
Ft. Lauderdale, Florida

Kate Boehm Nyquist
Science Writer and Curriculum Specialist
Mount Pleasant, South Carolina

Dr. Karen L. Ostlund
Professor
Science Education Center
The University of Texas at Austin
Austin, Texas

Contributing Authors

Dr. Anna Uhl Chamot
*Associate Professor and
ESL Faculty Advisor*
Department of Teacher Preparation
  and Special Education
Graduate School of Education
  and Human Development
The George Washington University
Washington, D.C.

Dr. Jim Cummins
Professor
Modern Language Centre and
  Curriculum Department
Ontario Institute for Studies in Education
Toronto, Canada

Gale Phillips Kahn
Lecturer, Science and Math Education
Elementary Education Department
California State University, Fullerton
Fullerton, California

Vince Sipkovich
Teacher
Irvine United School District
Irvine, California

Steve Weinberg
Science Consultant
Connecticut State Department
  of Education
Hartford, Connecticut

ISBN 0-673-59348-7

Copyright © 2000, Addison-Wesley Educational Publishers, Inc.

Printed in the United States of America

4567890 PO 03 02 01 00

Table of Contents

Scott Foresman *SCIENCE*
Activities Lab Manual

The goal of science education is to facilitate the development of skills, attitudes, and understandings that children will need in a rapidly changing society. To develop ideas, students need opportunities to interpret information, draw different inferences, and test ideas. This development can take place only *inside* the mind, not *outside* it. The process begins with observation, which is a mental activity, not just a response of the sense organs to stimuli. Observation skills are developed to enable students to use all the senses, appropriately and safely, to gather relevant information for investigations of things around them.

It is often implied that a scientific way of working is to start by collecting data and then to look for patterns. In reality, scientists may have a hypothesis in mind that determines what data are to be collected, and only a limited range of patterns can be found relating to that hypothesis. However, opportunities should be taken to use patterns to make predictions that can be checked. Inferences go further than looking for patterns—inferences suggest relationships that account for the patterns.

Questions are the means by which students can fill in some links between one experience and another and can make sense of the world. Once students embark on answering questions, others inevitably occur; and since further questions are generated in the context of the activity, it is likely that students will frame many of them in terms of what they can do themselves. Once begun, the process of defining testable questions is self-generating. Students soon realize from experience what kind of questions they can and cannot answer. Young children think out what to do in the course of doing it; they do not anticipate the result of actions, unless the actions are already familiar to them. Devising and conducting an investigation are interwoven, and young children may plan no further than the first step and from its result think what to do next.

If science is presented as a collection of facts, concepts, and laws, students are left with the perception that everything to be known about science has already been discovered and can be found in their textbook. This misrepresents the nature of science. Science is constantly changing. As research is conducted and advanced technology enhances the ability to make observations, scientific understanding of the world is modified. An awareness of the fluid nature of science helps students recognize that change is the rule rather than the exception. Science as a *process of inquiry* guides students to comprehend its dynamic nature.

Hands-on and minds-on experiences are fundamental to the inquiry approach to science. Teaching science as inquiry involves shifting from dependence on the textbook as the basic source of information to use of the textbook as a reference. Laboratory activities are central as students investigate and inquire about the world. Their own observations become the authoritative source of data. Students discover the facts, concepts, and laws of science in much the same way as the original discoverers did. The emphasis on firsthand observations in learning science reflects the belief that students should learn facts and concepts by modeling the processes used by scientists.

This discovery approach places greater emphasis on the logical thinking processes by which new knowledge is acquired and less emphasis on the rote learning of information. With the rapid rate at which knowledge is expanding, it is becoming difficult to prescribe exactly *which* facts and concepts should be transmitted to elementary students. It makes more sense to teach students the processes of science so that they can construct their own knowledge.

This program promotes the inquiry process through three types of activities—**Explore, Investigate,** and **Experiment.** The purpose and goals of each type of activity include:

Explore Activity

- Using all of their senses, and observing many different aspects of a new situation.

- Recording their observations with an increasingly rich descriptive vocabulary and/or more detailed pictures.

- Comparing observations with what they see or with what they know, and categorizing new objects and events as a way of making sense of phenomena.

- Recognizing some object or event as something that they had not seen before, and describing their new discovery in a way that is clear and convincing.

- Recording observations in a way that shows changes over an extended period of time.

- Going beyond simple observations to form questions and hypotheses that might become the basis for later investigations.

- Making inferences that may be speculative but are supported with evidence.

Investigate Activity

- Articulating a question—something they wonder about or a challenge they'd like to try.

- Devising and articulating a plan to answer their question or challenge.

- Carrying out their plan.

- Observing and evaluating the results of their plan.

- Modifying their plan as necessary.

- Exhibiting the important scientific attitudes of curiosity and persistence in pursuing their questions and challenges.

- Demonstrating an understanding of the science concepts involved in the phenomena being investigated.

- Solving problems and using other process skills in this investigative context.

Experiment Activity

- Formulating a hypothesis and comparing activity results to that hypothesis.

- Describing the variables in a situation.

- Designing a comparison situation in which all variables are controlled except the test variable.

- Conducting a controlled experiment—making observations, collecting data, analyzing data, and communicating results.

- Determining appropriate experimental outcomes.

- Drawing conclusions based on experimental results.

PROCESS SKILLS FOR SCIENCE INQUIRY

The inquiry/process skills are ways of thinking in science. When scientists and students engage in science activities, they are using critical thinking skills such as making accurate observations; comparing and contrasting; classifying; finding causes, reasons, and conclusions; predicting; generalizing; forming If … then arguments; communicating; and reasoning by analogy. The inquiry/process skills, along with the knowledge gained using those skills, and the scientific values and habits of mind define the nature of science. When students are actively engaged in hands-on/minds-on science activities, they learn more than facts and terminology. The **National Science Education Standards** (NSES) argue that *less is more,* suggesting that it is more beneficial to focus on fewer concepts than to cover enormous amounts of abstract science content. Hands-on activities can lead to minds-on understanding when students concentrate on a more manageable number of big ideas and are given adequate time to think about what they are learning.

The vision presented by the **NSES** describes inquiry as the "processes of science" requiring students to combine processes and scientific knowledge as they use scientific reasoning and critical thinking to develop their understanding of science. The standards state that inquiry is a "controlling principle in the ultimate organization and selection of students' activities." As students focus on the processes of doing investigations, they should have opportunities to describe objects and events; ask questions; construct explanations; test those explanations against current scientific knowledge; and communicate ideas to others.

Overall, the goals in teaching science should be to foster an attitude of inquiry, instill a feeling for the nature and processes of science, and develop an understanding of how science fits in the world around us. The challenge for classroom teachers, then, is to balance these goals.

One of the most important goals of education is to teach students to think. Although all school subjects should share in accomplishing this goal, science contributes the inquiry/process skills with emphasis on observing, hypothesizing, and interpreting data. The processes of science are broadly transferable abilities, appropriate to many science disciplines and reflective of the behavior of scientists.

The inquiry/process skills are the essence of the scientific method, which is a systematic approach to problem solving. The methods used to solve science problems can be used to solve many other kinds of problems. They are also methods that, once learned, can be applied in real-life situations. Learning inquiry/process skills will help students become better able to solve problems they encounter in their daily lives.

According to the **NSES,** the science curriculum should emphasize inquiry/process skills.

In general, research indicates that students will acquire these inquiry skills best if the processes of science are incorporated into the science program, infused in well-planned activities, and emphasized to students. Ideally, the activities stressing these inquiry/process skills will allow students to freely explore science concepts. Many science educators believe that activities offering the greatest possible benefit to students will be open-ended; that is, structured so that numerous responses may be acceptable or so there is more than one acceptable method of solving the problem identified. Activities in which there is no *one* right answer, or no apparent predetermined answer, may be most beneficial to developing students' abilities.

Research studies focusing on inquiry-based science programs indicate that when taught the inquiry/process skills, elementary school students not only learn to use those processes but also retain them for future use. Students are more likely to learn the processes of science when such skills are considered an important objective of instruction and proven teaching methods are used.

Scott Foresman *SCIENCE* balances the teaching of science content and the inquiry/process skills through numerous hands-on activities included in the student text. The program provides developmentally appropriate activities that help elementary students learn to use and apply the inquiry/process skills. The Teacher's Edition includes a **Skills Trace** identifying when a specific process skill is introduced, applied, and assessed.

The **Explore, Investigate,** and **Experiment** activities provide students with an opportunity to apply science concepts to interesting, motivational hands-on/minds-on experiences. Each activity gives students practice with specific inquiry/process skills. In keeping with research findings, the skill emphasized is noted in the student text as well as the Teacher's Edition.

The **Performance Assessments** at the end of each unit require students to apply the processes of inquiry. The processes used in each Performance Assessment are listed in the Teacher's Edition. Record sheets to accompany each performance assessment are included in the **Lab Manual** ancillary.

SCIENCE PROCESS SKILLS LESSONS/ACTIVITIES

The Student's Edition discusses the importance of the inquiry/process skills. It describes scientific methods as a systematic approach to problem solving using inquiry/process skills. The **Lab Manual** includes a *Science Process Skills* section with activities that use ordinary, accessible materials. These activities are designed to teach and reinforce the process skills. The Science Process Skills section also provides background information for the teacher, pre-activity discussion questions, and an extension activity.

The program also includes Science Process Skills blackline masters to accompany each process skill activity. These activities offer hands-on practice using the processes of science. The program provides ample opportunities for students to experience and practice inquiry/process skills.

One of the advantages of teaching inquiry/process skills in the science curriculum is that the activities require that each student participate cognitively in the learning process.

The science process skills used in this program are described in the following list. It is interesting to note that many of these processes of science relate to the critical thinking skills used throughout the program. This does not mean that the critical thinking skills and the processes of science are the same; rather, it is likely that as students use particular processes, they will also use particular critical thinking skills, and a pattern may emerge to link these two different types of skills.

Observing—the use of the five senses to gather data about objects and events

Communicating—the use of spoken and written words, graphs, drawings, and diagrams to share information and ideas with others

Classifying—grouping objects or events according to similar properties

Predicting—the use of data to forecast future events based on observations and inferences

Estimating and Measuring—an indirect means of measuring that involves making mental comparisons and calculations followed by the use of standard or nonstandard units to determine length, mass, volume, time, etc.

Inferring—the use of a logical thought process to show a relationship between observations or to explain an observation

Making Operational Definitions—writing a definition framed in terms of one's experiences

Making and Using Models—developing a conceptual or physical representation of an object or event

Formulating Questions and Hypotheses—making educated guesses that can be tested experimentally about the relationship of manipulated and responding variable

Collecting and Interpreting Data—gathering information through observations and measurements and determining its usefulness

Identifying and Controlling Variables—identifying and controlling variables to determine their effect on the outcome of an experiment

Experimenting—hypothesizing, designing an experiment to test a hypothesis, controlling variables, interpreting the data collected, and drawing conclusions

Teaching the inquiry/process skills gives students a "feel" for the nature of science and enables students to do science. Thus, students learn the content of science by doing science, which gives them a better understanding of the nature of science. Inquiry/process skills are not isolated bits of knowledge. Students may forget facts such as the boiling point of water, but once they learn how to measure temperature, they will never forget how to perform this inquiry/process skill.

What Is Performance-Based Assessment?

Traditional and standardized tests have often been criticized for failing to measure what students can actually do with their knowledge and skills. Traditional tests tend to emphasize acquisition of knowledge and skills rather than how they are used. Today, nontraditional forms of assessment have been designed and developed in science. These tests assess and evaluate student performance. They indicate how effectively students are using their knowledge and skills. Students are assessed on their ability to solve problems and perform tasks using good judgment, demonstrating accuracy of knowledge, and displaying mastery of skills. Components of performance assessment include involvement of a real-world setting, solution of open-ended problems with the possibility of alternative solutions, active participation by students as in the manipulation of materials and equipment, and a focus on ideas that are central to the main themes of science. Nontraditional performance assessments require students to use their skills in order to demonstrate their performance on tasks and to emphasize knowledge and thinking processes.

Performance-Based Assessment Tasks

Performance assessment tasks can be used to assess students at the end of a year. They can also serve as the foundation of instructional units. Used throughout the year, these tasks can be related to activities, monitor student progress, and provide feedback about that progress. Performance assessments that take place throughout the school year give students practice in the kinds of tasks they may be expected to do in a year-end performance assessment or to do eventually in real life. Doing such practice tasks helps students prepare for the culminating task, which may be a statewide or schoolwide form of performance assessment. Results of practice sessions can be recorded to show students' patterns of response over time.

Performance Assessment Strategies

Several types of performance assessment tests have been designed. In one type, students are presented with much of the specific content needed to complete the task. They are then asked to use the information in some way, such as analyzing and drawing conclusions from graphs or diagrams, completing projects, designing experiments, and evaluating situations. The students' responses may be indicated in a multiple-choice format. Another type of test requires students to complete a task or tasks within a short time by manipulating objects and analyzing or drawing conclusions based on the data collected. Still another type involves long-term tasks that may continue through the study of a unit or throughout the school year: activities that occur in the regular science curriculum can help students complete the task.

Scott Foresman *SCIENCE* provides a nontraditional, performance-based activity for each unit. Performance-based activities are designed to assess the students' ability to observe, manipulate, measure, record, collect and analyze data, and apply concepts from the text. They provide the student with hands-on, problem-solving opportunities.

Real-World Assessment

The performance-based activity for each unit in grades 1–6 begins with a scenario grounded in a real-world context. The scenario presents students with a problem to solve that relates to the important concepts of the unit. For each activity there are two (grades 1–2) or three (grades 3–6) testing stations. Each station presents tasks that relate to the problem. Students move from station to station, using their skills and ability in scientific methodology to manipulate scientific tools and to collect and record data. Working individually, students spend 10 minutes at each station. There a card pictures the materials and equipment students will use at the station to perform the task and collect data. Following the equipment manipulation and data collection at the stations, students return to their desks to analyze and summarize their observations and the data they have collected.

The performance-based activities in **Scott Foresman** *SCIENCE* are easy to set up and require a minimum amount of equipment. Materials needed are easily obtainable; many will already be in the classroom for use in regular science activities.

How to Set Up and Administer Performance-Based Activities

Use a large desk or tabletop and a chair at each station. You can set up the stations in a separate room or in the classroom. If the stations are in the classroom, provide visual barriers to set them apart from the rest of the room. If possible, screen the stations from each other. Screens can be made from cardboard, tagboard, or wood. Set up the stations in a place with enough space so students can move easily from one station to another, where other students will not be disturbed, and where needed science materials are easily available. Note that each student will take about 10 minutes at each station, or about 1/2 hour to complete work at all stations. Only one student works at a station at a time. Students will do the Data Analysis section at their desks. If you have enough space, tables, and materials, prepare more than one set of stations. Then the class will complete the assessment more quickly.

A setup card is pictured on the teacher's **How to Set Up** section for each station. You may want to enlarge these pictures on a copy machine and laminate them so they can be reused. Place the appropriate card for reference at each station. Materials at each station should be arranged as shown on the setup card. A materials list and suggestions for station preparation are on the teacher's How to Set Up page for each station. Make sure enough consumable materials are available. Equipment and supplies for the activities are listed for each station.

Set up the stations beforehand. You might have students read the scenario for the unit aloud together. Discuss terminology to ensure that all students understand all the words used in the scenario. Provide each student with a copy of the Data Collection and Analysis sheet for the activities. Tell students to read and follow the directions on the sheet. Do not provide information about how to use the materials and equipment in performing the activities; properly using materials and equipment is part of the evaluation of students' performance. Students should have had experience using measurement and other skills.

Tell students to bring a pencil and their Data Collection and Analysis sheet to the stations. Be sure students understand they are to take turns, work independently, and not watch others or discuss their performance. Stress the importance of returning equipment to the positions shown on the setup card when they finish

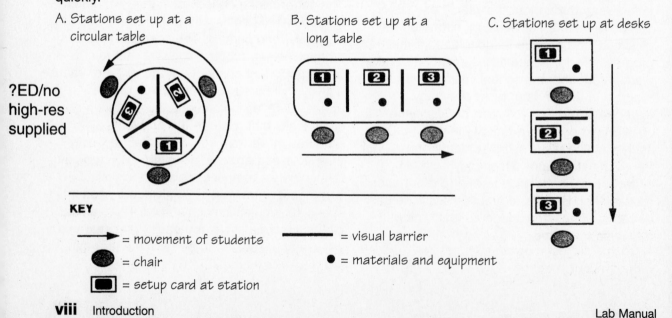

A. Stations set up at a circular table

B. Stations set up at a long table

C. Stations set up at desks

?ED/no high-res supplied

KEY

→ = movement of students   —— = visual barrier

⬤ = chair   ● = materials and equipment

▣ = setup card at station

work at a station. Allow students time to do this. Ask students to check the card before they start working at a station to be sure equipment is set up properly. Tell them where to find and dispose of consumable materials they might use, and ask them to move to the next station when you point out that 10 minutes are up. Tell students that when they finish the task at the three stations, they should return to their desks to complete the data analysis section of the test.

How to Evaluate the Performance-Based Activities

Before rating the students' performance, you should carefully review the station tasks, the analysis question (grades 3–6), and the criteria provided for them on the Evaluation Guide pages. The purpose statement with each Evaluation Guide section indicates what is being evaluated. When you clearly understand the tasks and the rating criteria, you can begin to evaluate students' answers on their data collection sheets.

When rating the students' responses (grades 3–6), you can give 3, 2, or 1 point for each station. Give 3, 2, or 1 point for the analysis question. A total score from 0 to 12 points is possible for each unit. Criteria for awarding points for each station and the analysis question are on the Evaluation Guide pages. Generally,

in rating the work at a station, give 3 points for a complete and correct response to the problem presented; give 2 points for a partial or partially correct response to the problem; and 1 point for attempting the work even though the response is incomplete or not completely correct. In scoring an analysis question, give 3 points for a response that relates the analysis of data and observations to concepts presented in the unit; give 2 points for a response that analyzes data but does not relate and apply concepts; and give 1 point for no response, an inappropriate response, or a response that does not analyze the data.

As you read each student's answer, keep in mind the task and the rating criteria. Assign each student the appropriate number of credits for each station and the analysis question, according to the criteria on the Evaluation Guide. Record the number of credits you give for each task in the margin of each student's answer sheet.

If possible, you might want to observe the students as they work at the stations and evaluate their performance. Rate the students only on their performance of the task and on the content of their responses. It is suggested that you do not reduce their scores for any incorrect grammar, spelling, or punctuation in written responses.

How to Use the Activity Scoring Rubrics in Scott Foresman *SCIENCE*

James E. Marshall and Adrienne L. Herrell
California State University, Fresno

Hands-on science activities, like many of those in **Scott Foresman** *SCIENCE*, often allow for multiple approaches to investigation and problem solving and even multiple correct answers. While these activities can elicit important information about the acquisition of knowledge and skills, they pose particular difficulties for equitable grading. These difficulties can be overcome by incorporating the use of "rubrics" in the grading process.

Rubrics are used as criteria by which an activity can be graded. Using a rubric serves as an effective teaching strategy by giving students a visible standard by which the activity will be judged. Students should be made familiar with the self-assessment checklist before they complete the activity. Students can review the checklist before turning in the activity. The checklist matches the teacher's scoring rubric which is found as a reduced page in the

Teacher's Edition and as a class record sheet on the (T) pages of the teacher's **Lab Manual**.

Each standard relates to one of four criteria—the procedure, the recording of data, the process skill(s) used, and the conclusions reached. The science process skills are included in the assessment as well as the student's understanding of the science content evident in the conclusions reached.

The rubric should be used with the students before they do the activity. The criteria should be discussed and examples given as to how each criteria can be met. Students need to thoroughly understand how they will be scored before the rubric is used to help them judge the level to which they are meeting the criteria as they complete the self-assessment checklist. Rubrics should be used for scoring each hands-on activity in the program. The scores can then be recorded using the class record sheets on (T) pages at the front of the book. Because the rubrics include the scoring of both science content knowledge and science process, the scores can be used to compute grades as well as to assess the student's progress in attaining these skills.

Self-Assessment Checklist	
I followed instructions to **observe** the parts of a plant.	_____
I made drawings and recorded **observations** of the stems and leaves of the plant.	_____
I removed the plant from the pot and made drawings and recorded observations of the roots.	_____
I repotted the plant.	_____
I **compared** and **contrasted** my observations with those of other groups.	_____

Self-Assessment Checklist	
I followed instructions to **observe** three stages in the life cycle of a beetle.	_____
I properly cared for the beetles.	_____
I **recorded** and drew my observations.	_____
I stated how long the stages in the development of the beetle lasted.	_____
I **compared** and **contrasted** the three stages of the beetle life cycle that I observed.	_____

Teaching Safety in the Classroom

Dr. Jack A. Gerlovich, Science Education Safety Consultant/Author
Des Moines, Iowa

Activities throughout **Scott Foresman** *SCIENCE* reinforce and extend science concepts using materials and procedures that are inherently safe. **Scott Foresman** *SCIENCE* teaches that safe procedure is part of sound scientific inquiry. Students who use this program learn not only how to safely investigate the topics at hand but also to develop safety habits that will serve them well in future scientific endeavors.

How does **Scott Foresman** *SCIENCE* accomplish this task? First and foremost, by performing the activities in the text, students learn that simple, safe materials can be used extensively to investigate science concepts. Second, safety reminders regarding procedure are given in the student text wherever appropriate. These include an exclamation point symbol and Safety Note statements on appropriate pages. Third, the Teacher's Edition includes safety tips for the various student activities and teacher demonstrations that appear throughout the program. Following is a list of the most general tips for the elementary/middle school science classroom. If followed from the start, these guidelines should be easily assimilated into classroom procedures by teachers and students alike.

- Demonstrate to students the proper use of safety goggles that meet American National Standards Institute (ANSI Z87.1) standards. Safety goggles should be worn whenever the potential for eye injury exists, for example, when heating any substance, when using any chemicals including "ordinary" substances such as vinegar, and when using glassware. Even relatively safe items such as rubber bands and balloons can cause eye injury and warrant the use of goggles.

- To prevent student interference with each other and to assist the safe exit of students from the room in case of an emergency, try to assure that rooms are not overcrowded, students understand exit procedures, and aisles are kept uncluttered.

- Periodically conduct simulations with students for dealing with foreseeable emergencies. Examples might include exiting the room because of an emergency, coping with a fire, aiding someone who has been splashed by a substance, and helping a person who has fallen.

- Before using any equipment or substances, be certain that you understand the proper function and hazards associated with the use of those items. Communicate this information to students.

- Unless you know the outcome is safe, never mix substances "just to see what happens." Scott Foresman SCIENCE does not use any hazardous substances. However, the combining of certain substances might pose safety problems. For example, mixing ammonia with bleach produces particularly dangerous fumes. Notes about the dangers of mixing chemicals are included on the appropriate pages throughout the program.

- Properly store all equipment. Keep the more dangerous items under lock and key.

- Whenever possible, use plastic items rather than glass. If glass containers are essential, select temperature- and break-resistant glassware.

- To prevent slipping and falls, wipe up any liquids spilled on tile or hardwood floors immediately.

- If you are not satisfied that all foreseeable dangers have been reduced to an acceptable level, alter or eliminate the activity.

Teachers should be aware of all applicable federal, state, and local regulations and relevant guidelines from professional organizations that apply to the activities being performed.

Examples include Occupational Safety and Health Administration (**OSHA**) standards for workplace safety; state laws relating to use of safety goggles; local fire department requirements regarding the use of open flame, fire extinguishers, and fire blankets; and National Science Teachers Association (**NSTA**) suggestions regarding overcrowding. Refer to the following materials for additional information about classroom safety.

Downs, G., et al. *Science Safety for Elementary School Teachers.* Ames, Iowa: Iowa State University Press, 1983.

Gerlovich, J., and K. Hartman. *Safe Science Teaching: A Diskette for Elementary Educators.* Waukee, Iowa: Jakel, Inc., 1990.

Scoring Key

4 correct, complete, detailed

3 partially correct, complete, detailed

2 partially correct, complete, lacks some detail

1 incorrect or incomplete, needs assistance

Explore Activity (p. A6)
Exploring Life Characteristics

Scoring Criteria

Student followed instructions to observe a mixture of yeast, sugar, and water.

Student followed instructions to observe a mixture of sand, sugar, and water.

Student recorded observations of the contents of the bottle and the balloons.

Student made inferences about whether sand or yeast was living.

Student listed the signs of life that were observed.

Score | total points | % equivalent

Investigate Activity (p. A22)
Observing Growth of Fungi

Scoring Criteria

Student followed instructions to observe mold growth on different foods.

Student collected data by recording observations of mold growth.

Student interpreted data by comparing and contrasting mold growth on different foods.

Student communicated by comparing and contrasting results with results of other students.

Student made inferences about how molds get energy and why mold can grow in the dark.

Score | total points | % equivalent

Scoring Key

4 correct, complete, detailed	**3** partially correct, complete, detailed	**2** partially correct, partially complete, lacks some detail	**1** incorrect or incomplete, needs assistance

Explore Activity (p. A38)

Exploring Cells

Scoring Criteria

Student followed instructions to observe the cells of an onion.

Student followed instructions to observe the cells of an elodea plant.

Student made drawings of observations.

Student compared and contrasted the onion and elodea cells.

Student made an inference about plant cells.

Score	
total points	
% equivalent	

Investigate Activity (p. A48)

Investigating the Life Cycle of a Flowering Plant

Scoring Criteria

Student followed directions to grow and pollinate a radish plant.

Student recorded observations.

Student measured the height of the plant.

Student collected and interpreted data and described the plant's development.

Student predicted what would happen to the new seeds if they were planted.

Score	
total points	
% equivalent	

4 correct, complete, detailed

3 partially correct, complete, detailed

2 partially correct, complete, lacks some detail

1 incorrect or incomplete, needs assistance

Investigate Activity (p. A58)

Investigating Dominant and Recessive Traits

Scoring Criteria

Student followed instructions to make a model of inheritance of flower color in plants.

Student made observations of the frequency of appearance of flower colors in a model.

Student determined the color of offspring produced when one parent is hybrid.

Student determined the color of offspring produced when both parents are hybrid.

Student made inferences about dominant and recessive inherited traits.

Score | total points
| % equivalent

Experiment Activity (p. A67)

Surveying Inherited Traits

Scoring Criteria

Student made a hypothesis about forms of traits.

Student identified and controlled variables.

Student followed instructions to conduct a survey to test a hypothesis.

Student collected and interpreted data by making a chart of observations and making and studying a graph.

Student communicated by stating conclusions.

Score | total points
| % equivalent

Scoring Key

4 correct, complete, detailed	**3** partially correct, complete, detailed	**2** partially correct, partially complete, lacks some detail	**1** incorrect or incomplete, needs assistance

Explore Activity (p. A74)
Exploring Protective Coloring

Scoring Criteria

Student followed instructions to construct a moth habitat model.

Student observed the moths and recorded predictions about which would be picked up.

Student recorded the number of each type of moth the team picked up.

Student determined which type of moth was picked up more often.

Student made an inference about protective coloration in moths.

Score

total points	
% equivalent	

Investigate Activity (p. A88)
Investigating Eggshells

Scoring Criteria

Student followed instructions to test the strength of eggshells.

Student recorded observations of the strength of eggshells.

Student observed eggshells in vinegar and recorded observations.

Student explained how an eggshell is fragile or strong.

Student made an inference about how the shell helps the developing chick survive in its habitat.

Score

total points	
% equivalent	

Activity Rubrics
Unit A Chapters 3–4

Scoring Key

4 correct, complete, detailed

3 partially correct, complete, detailed

2 partially correct, partially complete, lacks some detail

1 incorrect or incomplete, needs assistance

Investigate Activity (p. A96)

Investigating Insulation

Scoring Criteria

Student followed instructions to make and use a model of fat insulation.

Student recorded predictions and observations.

Student compared predictions with results.

Student explained why shortening is a good or poor insulator.

Student explained why fat is important to Arctic animals.

| Score | total points |
| | % equivalent |

Explore Activity (p. A108)

Exploring Parts of Soil

Scoring Criteria

Student followed instructions to observe soil samples.

Student recorded descriptions.

Student communicated by writing a one-sentence summary about each group observed.

Student classified the contents of soil sample as living, once-living, or nonliving.

Student described the appearance of the nonliving parts of the soil.

| Score | total points |
| | % equivalent |

Scoring Key

4 correct, complete, detailed	**3** partially correct, complete, detailed	**2** partially correct, partially complete, lacks some detail	**1** incorrect or incomplete, needs assistance

Investigate Activity (p. A116)

Investigating Owl Pellets

Scoring Criteria

Student followed instructions to examine an owl pellet.

Student recorded observations of the owl pellet and its contents.

Student made an inference about the owl's niche in its ecosystem.

Student made an inference about the food the owl eats.

Student made an inference about the food eaten by the owl's prey.

Score	total points
	% equivalent

Experiment Activity (p. A135)

Experimenting with Carbon Dioxide and Photosynthesis

Scoring Criteria

Student made a hypothesis about how light affects ability of a plant to use carbon dioxide.

Student identified and controlled variables.

Student followed instructions to perform an experiment to detect carbon dioxide.

Student collected and interpreted data from predictions and observations and chart study.

Student communicated by stating conclusion about light's effect on photosynthesis.

Score	total points
	% equivalent

Scoring Key

4 correct, complete, detailed

3 partially correct, complete, detailed

2 partially correct, partially complete, lacks some detail

1 incorrect or incomplete, needs assistance

Explore Activity (p. B6)

Exploring Elements

Scoring Criteria

Student followed instructions to observe objects made of one or more elements.

Student described each object and recorded observations.

Student classified the objects by their properties.

Student listed the properties used to classify the objects.

Student communicated by discussing how elements were classified with the class.

Score | total points | % equivalent

Investigate Activity (p. B22)

Investigating Water

Scoring Criteria

Student followed instructions to separate water into the elements it is made of.

Student recorded observations of the pencil tips as electric current flowed through water.

Student recorded observations of the pencil tip as the electric current stopped flowing.

Student stated evidence that electric current can separate water into the elements it is made of.

Student made an inference about the elements produced at each pencil point.

Score | total points | % equivalent

Scoring Key

4 correct, complete, detailed	**3** partially correct, complete, detailed	**2** partially correct, partially complete, lacks some detail	**1** incorrect or incomplete, needs assistance

Investigate Activity (p. B38)

Investigating a Chemical Change

Scoring Criteria

Student followed instructions to make a chemical change occur.

Student made predictions about what would happen when baking soda was added to water and to vinegar.

Student recorded observations.

Student made inferences about new substances being formed.

Student identified the combination that caused a chemical change to occur.

Score	total points
	% equivalent

Explore Activity (p. B44)

Exploring Motion

Scoring Criteria

Student followed instructions to construct a pendulum.

Student observed the motion of the pendulum.

Student controlled and changed the pendulum's motion.

Student explained how the motion of the pendulum was controlled and changed.

Student communicated by discussing observations of the pendulum's motion with the class.

Score	total points
	% equivalent

Activity Rubrics
Unit B Chapter 2

Scoring Key

4 correct, complete, detailed

3 partially correct, complete, detailed

2 partially correct, partially complete, lacks some detail

1 incorrect or incomplete, needs assistance

Investigate Activity (p. B54)
Investigating Force Used to Move Objects

Scoring Criteria

Student followed instructions to measure length of rubber band when moving objects.

Student recorded measurements when moving objects across a smooth and a rough surface.

Student compared the amount of stretch needed to move objects of different masses.

Student described how results changed when moving objects across a rough surface.

Student made inferences about the force needed to move objects across surfaces.

Score | total points | % equivalent

Investigate Activity (p. B60)
Investigating Friction

Scoring Criteria

Student followed instructions to demonstrate how friction affects different objects on a ramp.

Student recorded observations of the properties of the objects.

Student recorded measurements of the board height needed to move each object.

Student described properties of objects that affect how the objects slid down a ramp.

Student classified by ranking objects according to how much friction was demonstrated.

Score | total points | % equivalent

Scoring Key

4 correct, complete, detailed	3 partially correct, complete, detailed	2 partially correct, partially complete, lacks some detail	1 incorrect or incomplete, needs assistance

Experiment Activity (p. B69)

Experimenting with Balloon Rockets

Scoring Criteria

Student made a hypothesis about the size of a balloon's opening and distance it would travel.

Student identified and controlled variables and experimented to test hypothesis.

Student measured different sizes of balloon openings and distances the balloons travelled.

Student collected and interpreted data by making a chart and studying a graph.

Student communicated by stating conclusion.

Score	total points	% equivalent

Explore Activity (p. B76)

Modeling Roller Coaster Motion

Scoring Criteria

Student followed instructions to make and use a model roller coaster.

Student observed the movement of the marble on the model roller coaster.

Student made a drawing of model and marked where the marble sped up and slowed down.

Student described what had to be done to make the marble roll all the way over the hill.

Student made an inference about what caused changes in the marble's speed.

Score	total points	% equivalent

Activity Rubrics
Unit B Chapter 3

Scoring Key

4	correct, complete, detailed
3	partially correct, complete, detailed
2	partially correct, partially complete, lacks some detail
1	incorrect or incomplete, needs assistance

Investigate Activity (p. B84)
Investigating Potential Energy

Scoring Criteria

Student followed instructions to observe and measure the distance a marble can move a cup.

Student collected and interpreted data.

Student made predictions based on the data.

Student stated the relationship between the height of the ramp and the distance the marble moved the cup.

Student made inferences about the potential and kinetic energy of the marble and the amount of work done by the marble.

| Score | total points |
| | % equivalent |

Investigate Activity (p. B96)
Investigating Radiant Energy

Scoring Criteria

Student followed instructions to test how radiant energy affects light-sensitive paper.

Student recorded predictions and observations.

Student compared and contrasted the shapes produced on the light-sensitive paper.

Student stated which materials blocked the most and the least sunlight.

Student stated the evidence of an energy change observed.

| Score | total points |
| | % equivalent |

Scoring Key

4 correct, complete, detailed	**3** partially correct, complete, detailed	**2** partially correct, partially complete, lacks some detail	**1** incorrect or incomplete, needs assistance

Experiment Activity (p. B103)

Experimenting with Sunscreens

Scoring Criteria

Student made a hypothesis about effectiveness of sunscreens with different SPF values.

Student identified and controlled variables.

Student followed instructions to perform an experiment.

Student collected and interpreted data by classifying paper samples and ranking them from lightest to darkest.

Student communicated by reporting conclusion to the class.

Score	total points
	% equivalent

Explore Activity (p. B110)

Exploring Electric Charges

Scoring Criteria

Student followed instructions to make a charge tester.

Student tested objects rubbed with wool and recorded observations.

Student tested objects rubbed with plastic wrap and recorded observations.

Student listed objects that attracted and repelled the + tape and the – tape.

Student made an inference and described how charged objects act when brought near others.

Score	total points
	% equivalent

Scoring Key

4 correct, complete, detailed	**3** partially correct, complete, detailed	**2** partially correct, complete, lacks some detail	**1** incorrect or incomplete, needs assistance

Investigate Activity (p. B118)

Testing Electrical Conductivity

Scoring Criteria

Student followed instructions and used the picture to build a circuit.

Student recorded predictions, tested them with the circuit built, and recorded observations.

Student classified objects as conductors or insulators.

Student made an inference about objects that would or would not conduct electricity.

Student made an inference about insulation on electrical cords.

Score | total points
| % equivalent

Investigate Activity (p. B128)

Making a Dimmer Switch

Scoring Criteria

Student followed instructions to make a dimmer switch.

Student recorded observations.

Student described how the brightness of the bulb changed.

Student indicated on a drawing where the wire was placed when the bulb was brightest and dimmest.

Student made an inference about graphite as a conductor and insulator.

Score | total points
| % equivalent

Scoring Key

4 correct, complete, detailed	**3** partially correct, complete, detailed	**2** partially correct, partially complete, lacks some detail	**1** incorrect or incomplete, needs assistance

Investigate Activity (p. B136)

Making a Current Detector

Scoring Criteria

Student followed instructions to make a current detector.																	
Student observed the current detector when the magnet was moved inside the coil.																	
Student observed the current detector when it was connected to a battery.																	
Student recorded observations.																	
Student made an inference about current produced by the moving magnet and the current produced by the battery.																	

Score

total points																	
% equivalent																	

Explore Activity (p. C6)

Exploring a Model of the Earth's Layers

Scoring Criteria

Student followed instructions to make a model of Earth.																	
Student measured the layers of the model.																	
Student recorded observations about model.																	
Student compared the layers of model.																	
Student compared model to Earth.																	

Score

total points																	
% equivalent																	

Activity Rubrics
Unit C Chapter 1

Scoring Key

4 correct, complete, detailed

3 partially correct, complete, detailed

2 partially correct, partially complete, lacks some detail

1 incorrect or incomplete, needs assistance

Investigate Activity (p. C12)

Investigating Moving Continents

Scoring Criteria

Student observed continent outlines and modeled how they may have fit together.

Student used different colors to shade in mountains, coal and glacial deposits, and fossils on each continent.

Student correctly labeled and cut out the continents, and fit them together.

Student communicated by discussing similarities and differences between map and a world map.

Student described patterns on map.

Score | total points
| % equivalent

Investigate Activity (p. C28)

Investigating Weathering

Scoring Criteria

Student followed instructions to make a model of weathering.

Student recorded observations of the weathering of chalk by water and stones.

Student recorded observations of the weathering of chalk by acid in vinegar.

Student identified the weathering of the chalk as physical or chemical weathering.

Student compared and contrasted the chalk in the different cups.

Score | total points
| % equivalent

Scoring Key

| **4** correct, complete, detailed | **3** partially correct, complete, detailed | **2** partially correct, partially complete, lacks some detail | **1** incorrect or incomplete, needs assistance |

Experiment Activity (p. C35)

Experimenting with Crystal Formation

Scoring Criteria

Student made a hypothesis about the effect the rate of cooling has on size of crystals that form.

Student followed instructions to perform an experiment on crystal formation.

Student identified and controlled variables.

Student collected and interpreted data by observing and by measuring and recording the size of the crystals.

Student communicated by stating conclusion about effect of rate of cooling on crystal size.

Score	total points
	% equivalent

Explore Activity (p. C42)

Exploring Earth's Resources

Scoring Criteria

Student followed instructions to observe some of Earth's resources.

Student listed uses for the resources.

Student listed resources that could be completely used up, resources that could be replenished, and resources that could never be used up.

Student recorded the objects that were classified in each group.

Student communicated by discussing if each resource could be replenished or not.

Score	total points
	% equivalent

Scoring Key

4	correct, complete, detailed
3	partially correct, complete, detailed
2	partially correct, complete, lacks some detail
1	incorrect or incomplete, needs assistance

Investigate Activity (p. C54)

Investigating Water Pollution

Scoring Criteria

Student followed instructions to make and use a model of underground water pollution.

Student recorded observations about water pollution.

Student described how pollution on land can pollute underground and surface water.

Student inferred how landfills could contribute to water pollution.

Student compared and contrasted model to a real lake and its surrounding land.

Score | total points
| % equivalent

Investigate Activity (p. C68)

Investigating Air Pollution

Scoring Criteria

Student followed instructions to make an air pollution detector.

Student observed the particles on each card and recorded observations.

Student compared and contrasted the cards.

Student communicated by comparing and contrasting cards with those of other groups.

Student made an inference about pollution differences in different locations.

Score | total points
| % equivalent

Scoring Key

4 correct, complete, detailed	**3** partially correct, complete, detailed	**2** partially correct, partially complete, lacks some detail	**1** incorrect or incomplete, needs assistance

Explore Activity (p. C74)
Exploring How Sunlight Moves Water

Scoring Criteria

Student followed instructions to make the setup.

Student observed the pail a few times a day for 1 or 2 days.

Student recorded observations.

Student communicated by making drawings of what student thinks happened in the pail.

Student described the role of the sunlight in the setup.

Score	total points
	% equivalent

Investigate Activity (p. C82)
Investigating Sunlight and the Earth's Tilt

Scoring Criteria

Student followed instructions to model the orbit of the Earth.

Student observed the amount of light on the model.

Student recorded observations.

Student explained how Earth's tilt affects how directly light reaches different parts of the Earth.

Student made an inference about the position of the Earth when it is winter in the Northern Hemisphere.

Score	total points
	% equivalent

Activity Rubrics
Unit C Chapters 3–4

Scoring Key

4	correct, complete, detailed
3	partially correct, complete, detailed
2	partially correct, partially complete, lacks some detail
1	incorrect or incomplete, needs assistance

Investigate Activity (p. C88)
Investigating How a Greenhouse Works

Scoring Criteria

Student followed instructions to make a model of a greenhouse.

Student recorded temperature measurements of each container every ten minutes.

Student compared air temperatures in the containers before and after exposure to sunlight.

Student identified and controlled variables in the activity and discussed why that is important.

Student compared model to the greenhouse effect on Earth.

Score | total points

% equivalent

Explore Activity (p. C108)
Making a Model of the Solar System

Scoring Criteria

Student followed instructions to make models of the planets.

Student used the chart to find the correct size for each planet model.

Student measured each planet drawing to make sure it had the proper diameter.

Student arranged the planets in order of their position from the sun.

Student described how the Earth compares in size to Venus and Jupiter.

Score | total points

% equivalent

Scoring Key

4 correct, complete, detailed	**3** partially correct, complete, detailed	**2** partially correct, partially complete, lacks some detail	**1** incorrect or incomplete, needs assistance

Investigate Activity (p.C126)

Making a Spectroscope

Scoring Criteria

Student followed instructions to make a spectroscope.

Student made a prediction about what would be seen in the spectroscope.

Student observed light from a bulb through the spectroscope.

Student recorded prediction, observations, and made a drawing.

Student explained how diffraction grating in a spectroscope changes light from a light bulb.

Score	total points
	% equivalent

Investigate Activity (p.C136)

Investigating Lenses

Scoring Criteria

Student followed instructions to record observations of objects through convex lenses.

Student drew a diagram of a convex lens.

Student followed instructions to make a simple refracting telescope.

Student wrote an operational definition of a convex lens.

Student described how to make and use a simple refracting telescope.

Score	total points
	% equivalent

Activity Rubrics
Unit D Chapter 1

Scoring Key

4 correct, complete, detailed

3 partially correct, complete, detailed

2 partially correct, partially complete, lacks some detail

1 incorrect or incomplete, needs assistance

Explore Activity (p. D6)

Exploring Lung Volume

Scoring Criteria

Student followed instructions to form a bubble dome.

Student measured the diameter of bubble after it burst.

Student recorded measurements.

Student used information in the table to determine lung volume.

Student inferred why there may be differences in lung volume among students.

Score | total points | % equivalent

Investigate Activity (p. D14)

Making a Breathing Model

Scoring Criteria

Student followed instructions to make a model of the respiratory system.

Student recorded predictions and observations about the workings of the model.

Student compared predictions and observations.

Student compared and contrasted the model with the actual process of breathing.

Student made an inference about the advantage of having an especially strong diaphragm.

Score | total points | % equivalent

Scoring Key

4 correct, complete, detailed	**3** partially correct, complete, detailed	**2** partially correct, partially complete, lacks some detail	**1** incorrect or incomplete, needs assistance

Experiment Activity (p. D25)

Experimenting with Exercise and Carbon Dioxide

Scoring Criteria

Student made a hypothesis about exercise and exhaling carbon dioxide.

Student identified and controlled variables.

Student followed instructions to perform an experiment.

Student collected and interpreted data by making a chart and making and studying a graph.

Student communicated by stating conclusion.

Score	
total points	
% equivalent	

Explore Activity (p. D32)

Exploring How Diseases Spread

Scoring Criteria

Student followed instructions to model how some diseases can be spread.

Student observed handprints left on the four pieces of construction paper.

Student recorded observations.

Student described how shaking hands can spread germs from person to person.

Student made an inference about ways that germs can get on hands.

Score	
total points	
% equivalent	

Activity Rubrics
Unit D Chapter 2

Scoring Key

4	correct, complete, detailed
3	partially correct, complete, detailed
2	partially correct, partially complete, lacks some detail
1	incorrect or incomplete, needs assistance

Investigate Activity (p. D56)
Measuring Heart Rates

Scoring Criteria

Student followed instructions to measure resting heart rate and exercising heart rate.

Student collected data by recording measurements in a chart.

Student described how heart rate changed after exercise.

Student made an inference about why heart rate changed when Student exercised.

Student communicated by discussing possible reasons for variations in heart rates.

Score

total points

% equivalent

Scoring Criteria

Score

total points

% equivalent

Contents
Part 1: Activity Record Sheets

Name _____ Date _____

Exploring Life Characteristics

Explore

3. Record your **observations** of the contents of the bottles and of the balloons.

_____

_____

_____

_____

_____

_____

_____

_____

_____

Reflect

1. Make an **inference** to answer the following question: Which shows signs of life, the yeast or the sand? Explain.

The bottle with yeast undergoes changes that indicate yeast

is alive. The bottle with sand does not change.

_____

_____

_____

_____

_____

Name _____   Date _____

2. What signs of life did you observe in this activity?

Students may see the contents of the bottle with yeast forms bubbles and the volume of the mixture increases. This indicates growth. Yeast uses food (sugar) to grow and reproduce. The balloon inflates, which shows some type of change is happening in the bottle. In this case it is a waste product (carbon dioxide) given off by the living yeast.

Inquire Further

What would happen to the yeast cells if you did not add sugar to the water? Develop a plan to answer this or other questions you may have.

Students may plan to repeat the procedure without adding sugar to the yeast and water. Without sugar to use as food, the yeast will not have energy to grow and reproduce.

Self-Assessment Checklist	
I followed instructions to **observe** a mixture of yeast, sugar, and water.	_____
I followed instructions to **observe** a mixture of sand, sugar, and water.	_____
I recorded my observations of the contents of the bottle and the balloons.	_____
I made **inferences** about whether sand or yeast was living.	_____
I listed the signs of life I observed.	_____

 Notes for Home Your child explored what happens when yeast and sugar are mixed together.
Home Activity: With your child, look at the ingredients in a yeast bread recipe and discuss what causes the bread to rise.

Name _____ Date _____

Observing Growth of Fungi

Follow This Procedure

4. Record your observations in the chart.

Mold observations			
Day	Bread	Orange peel	Tomato
1			
2	Students should notice mold beginning to grow after 3–5 days. Molds generally appear to be powdery or fuzzy and may vary in color.		
3			
4			
5			
6			
7			

Interpret Your Results

1. Compare and contrast the mold growth on the different foods. Does the same kind of mold grow on different types of food? Does mold spread from one piece of food to the one next to it? Did any piece of food have more than one kind of mold on it?

Different food items provide growing conditions for different

types of molds. Students may see instances of mold

growing on only one type of food. Other molds may grow on

several foods. Different types of mold may grow very near

to each other without spreading to the adjoining food.

_____

_____

_____

Name _____ Date _____

3. Make an **inference** based on your data and observations to explain how you think molds get energy. Why do you think mold can grow in the dark?

Fungi such as mold cannot obtain energy from the sun, as plants do. They obtain energy from other living or dead organisms. They can grow in the dark because they do not utilize energy from the sun as green plants do.

Inquire Further

Could the molds grow without water? in a sunny spot? Develop a plan to answer these or other questions you may have.

Students may plan to set up a similar experiment, varying the water or light conditions.

Self-Assessment Checklist	
I followed instructions to **observe** mold growth on different foods.	_____
I **collected data** by recording my observations of mold growth.	_____
I **interpreted data** by comparing and contrasting mold growth on different foods.	_____
I **communicated** by comparing and contrasting my results with the results of other students.	_____
I made **inferences** about how molds get energy and why mold can grow in the dark.	_____

 Notes for Home Your child **observed** the growth of fungi.
Home Activity: Explain to your child that mold grows on the north side of trees and ask your child to speculate why.

Exploring Cells

Explore

4–5. Record your observations in the chart.

	Drawing of observations
Onion	**Student drawing should show small boxes with a dark spot in each. (The boxes are the cells and the spots are the nuclei.) A slight reddish color may be visible in the onion and green spots and coloration in the elodea.**
Elodea	

Reflect

1. Compare and contrast the cells of the onion and elodea plant.

The onion and elodea both have cells that are shaped like

small compartments with a dark spot in them. The elodea

also has green spots in the cells.

_____

_____

2. Make an **inference.** What other things might cells do for the plant besides making food?

Students may reply that plant cells may also be involved in transporting water and nutrients. In the case of the onion the cells observed are food storage cells.

Inquire Further

What do other cells look like? Develop a plan to answer this or other questions you may have.

Students may look at cells from various plant parts. Students may observe pond water to look for single-celled organisms and algae cells.

Self-Assessment Checklist	
I followed instructions to **observe** the cells of an onion.	_____
I followed instructions to **observe** the cells of an elodea plant.	_____
I made drawings of my observations.	_____
I compared and contrasted the onion and elodea cells.	_____
I made an **inference** about plant cells.	_____

Notes for Home Your child **observed** onion skin cells and elodea cells.
Home Activity: With your child, look at pictures of cells from other plants or animals and compare and contrast them to the cells from the onion and elodea.

Investigating the Life Cycle of a Flowering Plant

Use with pages A48–A49.

Follow This Procedure

3–4. Record your data and observations in the chart.

Date	Observations	Plant height	Drawing of plant

Interpret Your Results

1. Describe how the plant developed from the time you began to observe it until seeds were formed?

Students may want to describe 4 or 5 stages in the

development of the plant. Stages may include: sprout,

grown plant, flowering plant, fruiting plant, seed.

_____

_____

_____

_____

_____

Name _____ Date _____

2. **Predict** what would happen if you planted your seeds.

__Students should predict that their seeds would sprout, grow,__

__flower, and produce fruit. Actual germination of planted__

__seeds would vary if students were to test their predictions.__

_____

_____

_____

_____

_____

Inquire Further

Would the plant grow faster if you changed how much water or fertilizer you gave it? Develop a plan to answer this or other questions you may have.

__Students may wish to grow more radish plants with changes in__

__amounts of water, fertilizer, or other variables. Accept__

__reasonable plans.__

_____

_____

Self-Assessment Checklist

I followed directions to grow and pollinate a radish plant.	_____
I recorded my **observations.**	_____
I **measured** the height of the plant.	_____
I **collected** and **interpreted data** and described the plant's development.	_____
I **predicted** what would happen to the new seeds if I planted them.	_____

 Notes for Home Your child **observed** the stages in the life cycle of a flowering plant by growing and pollinating a radish plant.
Home Activity: Call a local nursery to find out what kind of fertilizer different plants need and why.

Name _____ Date _____

Investigating Dominant and Recessive Traits

Follow This Procedure

6–9. Record your observations in the chart.

Parents		Offspring	
	RR (red)	Rr (red)	rr (white)
RR x Rr			
Total			
Rr x Rr			
Total			

Interpret Your Results

1. How many red-flowered offspring and how many white-flowered offspring are produced when one parent has two genes for red flowers and one parent is hybrid?

Students should conclude that when a hybrid parent and a

parent with two genes for red flowers are bred, the offspring

would always have red flowers.

_____

_____

_____

2. How many red-flowered offspring and how many white-flowered offspring are produced when both parents are hybrid?

Students should conclude that when both parents are hybrid, approximately three out of four offspring would be red-flowered and one would be white-flowered.

3. What can you **infer** from your data about inheritance of dominant and recessive traits?

Students should infer that whenever a dominant gene is present in an offspring, the dominant trait will be observed.

Students should infer that recessive traits occur only when two recessive genes are present in the offspring.

Inquire Further

How would your results be different if you tossed a chip for a hybrid (Rr) and a chip for two recessive genes (rr)? Develop a plan to answer this or other questions you may have.

_____

_____

_____

Self-Assessment Checklist	
I followed instructions to **make a model** of inheritance of flower color in plants.	_____
I made **observations** of the frequency of appearance of flower colors in a model of plant reproduction and inheritance.	_____
I determined how many red-flowered and white-flowered offspring are produced when one parent has two genes for red flowers and one parent is hybrid.	_____
I determined how many red-flowered and white-flowered offspring are produced when both parents are hybrid.	_____
I made **inferences** about dominant and recessive inherited traits.	_____

Notes for Home Your child **investigated** the frequency of inheritance of genes and traits by making a model.

Home Activity: Follow the same procedure to model the frequency of inheritance of your child's eye color, hair color, or height.

Surveying Inherited Traits

State the Problem

Are some forms of inherited traits more common than others?

Formulate Your Hypothesis

Which form of each of the traits shown do you think is more common among students in your class? Write your **hypothesis.**

_____

_____

_____

_____

Identify and Control the Variables

Who you survey is a **variable** you can control. Use a sample of students, not just those who are your friends or who sit near you. Survey the same group of students for all the traits on your list. Try to survey at least 20 students.

Test Your Hypothesis

3. Record your data in the chart.

Collect Your Data

	Tally of students	Total
Can curl tongue	**Student data will vary**	**depending on the**
Cannot curl tongue	**individuals tested.**	
Unattached earlobe		
Attached earlobe		
Widow's peak		
No widow's peak		

Interpret Your Data

Use the data from your chart to make a bar graph.

Inherited Traits of Fifth Graders

Number of students

| 28 |
| 24 |
| 20 |
| 16 |
| 12 |
| 8 |
| 4 |
| 0 |

Can Curl tongue | Cannot curl tongue | Unattached earlobe | Attached earlobe | Widow's peak | No widow's peak

Traits

State Your Conclusion

How do your results compare with your hypothesis? **Communicate** your results. Explain how the occurrence of traits varies among the students you surveyed.

_____

_____

Inquire Further

If you surveyed a larger group of students, how would your results be affected? Develop a plan to answer this or other questions you may have.

Students may wish to survey an older age group. Dominant genes should show up in the same percentages across genders.

Self-Assessment Checklist	
I made a **hypothesis** about forms of traits.	_____
I **identified** and **controlled variables.**	_____
I followed instructions to conduct a **survey** to test my hypothesis.	_____
I **collected** and **interpreted data** by making a chart of my **observations** and making and studying a graph.	_____
I **communicated** by stating my conclusions.	_____

Notes for Home Your child **experimented** to see if some inherited traits are more common among students. **Home Activity:** Help your child survey family members and friends for the same traits; compare the results with those of the classroom experiment.

Name _____   Date _____

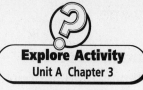

Exploring
Protective Coloring

Explore

3. Which will be picked up more often, the newspaper or the construction paper moths? Why? Record your **prediction** and explanation.

Students may predict that both will be picked up the

same amount because there are equal numbers of both

colors. Or students may predict that the black moths will

stand out more on the newspaper and therefore will be

picked up more often.

5. Count and record the number of each type of moth your team picked up.

Students should count more construction paper moths

picked up and more newspaper moths left behind.

Reflect

1. Was your prediction correct? Which type of moth was picked up more often?

Students should find that the black construction paper

moths were picked up more often.

2. Make an **inference** to answer the following question: Which moth would be more likely to survive in the newspaper habitat? Explain.

Students may infer that the newspaper moths would be

more likely to survive in the newspaper habitat because it

would be harder for predators to find them.

Inquire Further

What would happen if the habitat was black? Develop a plan to answer this or other questions you may have.

Students may use this same activity to test black moths and

newspaper (or another color of paper) moths on black

construction paper. Students should find similar results—

more black moths would be left behind while the newspaper

moths would be picked up more often.

Self-Assessment Checklist

I followed instructions to construct a moth habitat model.	_____
I **observed** the moths and recorded my **predictions** about which type of moth would be picked up more often.	_____
I recorded the number of each type of moth my team picked up.	_____
I determined which type of moth was picked up more often.	_____
I made an **inference** about protective coloration in moths.	_____

Notes for Home Your child explored how a moth's coloring protects it from being seen in its habitat.
Home Activity: Ask your child to name other animals whose coloring protects them from predators by helping them blend into their habitat.

Name _____ Date _____

Investigating Eggshells

Follow This Procedure

4, 6, and 7. Record your **observations** in the chart.

	Observations
Number of books to break eggshells	**Observations may vary depending on the weight of the books used.**
Eggshells in vinegar after five minutes	**Students should observe bubbles rising from the eggshells.**
Eggshells in vinegar overnight	**Eggshells should have dissolved or become very thin and fragile, but the inner membrane of the eggshells should still remain.**

Interpret Your Results

1. Do you think a chicken egg is fragile or strong? Explain.

Students may reply that the egg seems both fragile and strong: The dome shape makes the egg strong, but brittleness of shell makes it easy to break when it is in pieces.

2. Make an **inference** to answer the following question: How does the shell of an egg help a developing chick to survive in its habitat?

The shell protects the developing chick from some predators. It is sturdy enough for the female to incubate the egg without breaking it.

3. How does vinegar affect the calcium compound?

The acid in vinegar dissolves the calcium compound in

the eggshells.

_____

_____

Inquire Further

Does the size of the eggshell affect its strength? Develop a plan to answer this or other questions you may have.

Students may plan to test different-sized eggshells for

strength. Students can follow the procedure of this activity

to compare small, medium, large, and extra large eggshells.

Students should use the same books in the same order of

placement with each set of eggshells.

_____

_____

Self-Assessment Checklist	
I followed instructions to test the strength of eggshells.	_____
I recorded my **observations** of the strength of eggshells.	_____
I observed eggshells in vinegar and recorded my observations.	_____
I explained how an eggshell is fragile or strong.	_____
I made an **inference** about how the shell helps the developing chick survive in its habitat.	_____

Notes for Home Your child tested the strength of eggshells.
Home Activity: Help your child identify other objects made of calcium that are very strong.

Name _____ Date _____

Investigating Insulation

Follow This Procedure

Use with pages A96–A97.

6. Record your **prediction**, explanation, and **observations** in the chart.

	Shortening	No shortening
Prediction	Students may predict that hand with shortening will stay warmer in cold water. They may use	
Start	knowledge about fat layers to explain that fat insulates animals (shortening is fat). Shortening	
30 seconds	insulates and keeps hand warmer than empty	
1 minute	bags. Observations should be the same after 30 seconds and 1 minute.	

Interpret Your Results

1. Compare your prediction with your results.

_____

2. Do you think that shortening is a good or a poor insulator? Explain.

   Shortening is a good insulator. It keeps heat from escaping from the hand.

_____

_____

3. Why is the fatty layer on an Arctic animal important? Compare it to your model.

   Shortening works like the layer of fat beneath the skin of many Arctic animals. This layer of fat acts as insulation to keep body heat from being lost in freezing conditions.

_____

Inquire Further

What other materials can work as heat insulators? Develop a plan to answer this or other questions you may have.

<u>**Students may want to investigate other materials as**</u>

<u>**insulators such as wool, paper, cotton, fake fur, feathers, etc.**</u>

<u>**Depending on the materials, students could use the same**</u>

<u>**procedure for testing.**</u>

_____

_____

_____

_____

Self-Assessment Checklist	
I followed instructions to **make** and **use** a **model** of fat insulation.	_____
I recorded my **prediction** and **observations.**	_____
I compared my prediction with my results.	_____
I explained why I thought shortening is a good or poor insulator.	_____
I explained why fat is important to Arctic animals.	_____

 Notes for Home Your child investigated how Arctic animals stay warm by making a model of fat insulation.
Home Activity: Help your child identify other animals that have a fatty layer to keep them warm.

Exploring Parts of Soil

Explore

3. Describe three items in each group. Are there many like it, a few, or only one? Write a one-sentence summary of each group.

Answers will vary.

_____

_____

_____

_____

_____

_____

_____

Reflect

1. How did you classify items as living, once-living, or nonliving?

Living things—students probably searched for animals that moved. Once-living things—students probably selected bits of leaves, sticks, etc. They probably did not consider that living decomposers may grow on the once-living items. Nonliving things—students probably selected items that appeared to be tiny pieces of rock and sand.

2. Describe the appearance of the nonliving parts of the soil.

Students should describe small particles that look like broken or tiny rocks or sand.

_____

Inquire Further

If your soil was returned to the ground, what would happen to the once-living items over time? Develop a plan to answer this or other questions you may have.

Students may predict that once-living items would be used

as food by insects, worms, fungus, and bacteria that live in

the soil. They would eventually break down.

_____

_____

_____

_____

_____

Self-Assessment Checklist

I followed instructions to **observe** soil samples.	_____
I recorded my descriptions.	_____
I **communicated** by writing a one-sentence summary about each group I observed.	_____
I **classified** the contents of my soil sample as living, once-living, or nonliving.	_____
I described the appearance of the nonliving parts of the soil.	_____

Notes for Home Your child explored different materials found in soil.
Home Activity: Gather a handful of soil and ask your child to describe and classify the different materials for you.

Investigating Owl Pellets

Follow This Procedure

2–7. Record your **observations** in the chart.

	Observations
Outside of pellet	
Inside of pellet	
Teeth	
Skulls	

Interpret Your Results

1. Make an **inference.** What does the presence of fur and feathers tell you about the owl's niche in the ecosystem?

    The owl eats both mammals and birds. The owl is a

    predator in its habitat.

2. Make an **inference.** Based on your observations of skulls and bones, does the owl eat mostly one species of prey or several different species? Explain.

    Students may infer that the owl eats different species

    based on what the students find in the owl pellet.

3. Think about the types of teeth you found. Make an inference. What type or types of food are eaten by the owl's prey?

Its prey includes some animals that eat plants and some

that eat other animals.

_____

_____

_____

Inquire Further

How can you identify the species that the owl eats? Develop a plan to answer this or other questions you may have.

Students could compare the bones found with photos of

bones of the animals found in the owl's community. This

could lead to fairly accurate identification. Students may use

textbooks or field guides as references.

_____

_____

_____

_____

Self-Assessment Checklist	
I followed instructions to examine an owl pellet.	_____
I recorded my **observations** of the owl pellet and its contents.	_____
I made an **inference** about the owl's niche in its ecosystem.	_____
I made an **inference** about the food the owl eats.	_____
I made an **inference** about the food eaten by the owl's prey.	_____

Notes for Home Your child learned about an owl's niche in its ecosystem by studying owl pellets.
Home Activity: Use an encyclopedia or other reference book to investigate the type of teeth a mouse has and speculate about what a mouse might eat.

Name _____ Date _____

Experimenting with Carbon Dioxide and Photosynthesis

State the Problem

When a plant carries out photosynthesis it uses carbon dioxide. How does light affect the ability of a plant to use carbon dioxide?

Formulate Your Hypothesis

Will a plant exposed to light use more, less, or the same amount of carbon dioxide than a plant in the dark? Write your **hypothesis.**

_____

_____

_____

Identify and Control the Variables

The amount of light that the plants receive is the **variable** you can change. Keep the amount of bromothymol blue (BTB) solution, the length of the elodea, and the temperature the same.

Test Your Hypothesis

3. What happens when a person exhales through a straw into the BTB solution?

The color of the water in the cup turns greenish-yellow.

_____

5, 7–8. Record your predictions and observations in the chart.

Collect Your Data

Cup	Color at start	Predictions	Color after 30 minutes
A	**Predictions will vary. Some may predict that only**		
B	**plants in sunlight will not test for carbon dioxide;**		
C	**others may predict that both cups with plants will not show carbon dioxide. Students should observe a**		
D	**change of color in cup B.**		

Interpret Your Data

1. Which cup or cups still contained large amounts of carbon dioxide after 30 minutes?

   Cups A, C, and D still contained carbon dioxide.

2. Which cup or cups showed evidence that carbon dioxide had been used after 30 minutes?

   Cup B had less or no carbon dioxide present.

State Your Conclusion

How do your results compare with your hypothesis? Write what you conclude about how the presence or absence of light affects a plant's ability to use carbon dioxide.

Students should conclude that light needs to be present for a plant to use carbon dioxide and for photosynthesis to occur.

Inquire Further

What would happen if you allowed the cups to remain open for several hours or overnight? Develop a plan to answer this or other questions you may have.

Students should find that carbon dioxide may slowly escape from the solutions. All the solutions would turn or begin to turn blue.

Self-Assessment Checklist	
I made a **hypothesis** about how light affects the ability of a plant to use carbon dioxide.	_____
I **identified** and **controlled variables.**	_____
I followed instructions to perform an **experiment** using bromothymol blue to detect carbon dioxide in the cups.	_____
I **collected** and **interpreted data** by recording **predictions** and **observations** and by studying a chart.	_____
I **communicated** by stating my conclusion about how light affects a plant's ability to use carbon dioxide.	_____

Notes for Home Your child **experimented** to see how light affects the ability of a plant to use carbon dioxide.
Home Activity: Help your child find out why a poinsettia plant needs to be in the dark for its leaves to turn red.

Name _____ Date _____

Exploring Elements

Explore

2. Record your observations in the chart.

Object	Observations
Aluminum foil	
Penny	
Paper clip	
Graphite in a pencil	

3. Classify the objects into two groups and write the properties used to classify them beneath each group.

Group 1 Properties	Group 2 Properties

Reflect

1. Which properties did you use to classify the objects?

Possible answers: metal vs. nonmetal; shiny vs. dull; light color vs. dark color; or properties such as shape, ability to be bent, etc.

2. Would you classify the elements oxygen and nitrogen in one of your groups or would you use another group to classify them? Explain.

Students may answer that oxygen and nitrogen should be classified in a different group because they are invisible gases.

Inquire Further

What are some uses of the elements you observed? Develop a plan to answer this or other questions you may have.

Students may refer to textbooks, science encyclopedias, or other sources to find out how the elements are used.

_____

_____

_____

_____

Self-Assessment Checklist

I followed instructions to **observe** objects made of one or more elements.	_____
I described each object and recorded my observations.	_____
I **classified** the objects by their properties.	_____
I listed the properties I used to classify the objects.	_____
I **communicated** by discussing how I classified elements with the class.	_____

Notes for Home Your child observed and classified different materials.
Home Activity: Ask your child to classify different items in your home.

Investigating Water

Follow This Procedure

7–8. Record your observations in the chart.

	Observations
Electric current flowing	**Bubbles form at the pencil point.**
Electric current not flowing	**No bubbles form at the pencil point.**

Interpret Your Results

1. What evidence do you have that during this activity water was separated into hydrogen and oxygen?

   Bubbles formed at the points of the pencil when the circuit was closed, indicating that water separated into hydrogen and oxygen. When one pencil was removed from the water, the circuit was opened and bubbles did not form.

2. Make inferences to answer the following questions: At which pencil point was oxygen produced?

   Students may infer that oxygen was produced at the pencil point with fewer bubbles.

   At which pencil point was hydrogen produced? Explain.

   Students may infer that hydrogen was produced at the pencil point where more bubbles were produced because there are two atoms of hydrogen for every one atom of oxygen in water.

Name _____ Date _____

Inquire Further

Would the reaction work if you didn't add baking soda to the water? Develop a plan to answer this or other questions you may have.

Student plans may include repeating the experiment without
_____
adding baking soda to the water. They should find that the
_____
reaction occurs and bubbles form, but at a reduced rate.
_____

_____

_____

_____

_____

_____

Self-Assessment Checklist	
I followed instructions to separate water into the elements it is made of.	_____
I recorded my **observations** of the pencil tips as electric current flowed through water.	_____
I recorded my **observations** of the pencil tip as the electric current stopped flowing.	_____
I stated evidence that electric current can separate water into the elements it is made of.	_____
I made an **inference** about the elements produced at each pencil point.	_____

 Notes for Home Your child split water into the elements it is made of—oxygen and hydrogen.
Home Activity: Ask your child how he or she knew at which pencil point hydrogen was produced and at which pencil point oxygen was produced.

Name _____ Date _____

Investigating a
Chemical Change

Follow This Procedure

5 and 6.   Record your predictions and observations in the chart.

	Predictions	Observations
Baking soda and water	**Students may predict that the baking soda will mix or dissolve in the water.**	**The water becomes cloudy. Some baking soda may dissolve, some may settle to the bottom.**
Baking soda and vinegar	**Students may predict that bubbles or foam will form.**	**Bubbles and foam form, the balloon inflates.**

Interpret Your Results

1. Make an inference to answer the following question: When you combined baking soda and water, was there evidence of a new substance being formed? Explain.

   Students should infer that no new substance formed. The

   baking soda mixed with the water and some dissolved in

   the water, but there is no evidence of a new substance.

   _____

2. Make an inference to answer the following question: When you combined baking soda and vinegar, was there evidence of a new substance being formed? Explain.

   Students should infer that a new substance was formed.

   Bubbles and foam formed and the balloon inflated with the

   gas that was produced.

   _____

3. Which combination caused a chemical change to occur? Explain.

   A chemical change occurred when the baking soda and

   vinegar combined. A new substance, carbon dioxide

   gas, was formed.

   _____

Inquire Further

What do you think would happen to the solutions if you allowed them to evaporate? Develop a plan to answer this or other questions you may have.

   Student plans should include a way to allow each of the

   solutions to evaporate. When the baking soda and water

   evaporate, baking soda will be left behind; when the

   baking soda and vinegar solution evaporates, a new

   substance will be left behind.

   _____

   _____

Self-Assessment Checklist	
I followed instructions to make a chemical change occur.	_____
I made **predictions** about what would happen when baking soda was added to water and to vinegar.	_____
I recorded my **observations**.	_____
I made **inferences** about new substances being formed.	_____
I **identified** the combination that caused a chemical change to occur.	_____

Notes for Home Your child produced and identified a physical and a chemical change.
Home Activity: Ask your child to name two physical changes and two chemical changes that occur at home.

Exploring Motion

Explore

2. Observe the motion of the pendulum. When is it moving the slowest? the fastest?

The pendulum is at its slowest at the end of each swing.

The pendulum is at its fastest in midswing.

3. How many swings does it take for the pendulum to knock down all the dominoes?

Student answers will vary.

Reflect

1. What did you do to control and change the pendulum's motion? How did you change the direction of the motion?

Student answers will vary. They may describe various

movements of the pendulum (back and forth or circular).

Students will have to use different amounts of force and

release the pendulum in different directions to control

and change its motion.

Name _____ Date _____

Inquire Further

What would happen to the pendulum's motion if you used a shorter string to make the pendulum? Develop a plan to answer this or other questions you may have.

Student plans should include rebuilding the pendulum using a

shorter string. A pendulum with a shorter string will have a

shorter period (the pendulum will swing back and forth more

rapidly).

_____

_____

_____

_____

Self-Assessment Checklist	
I followed instructions to construct a pendulum.	_____
I **observed** the motion of the pendulum.	_____
I controlled and changed the pendulum's motion.	_____
I explained how I controlled and changed the motion of the pendulum.	_____
I **communicated** by discussing my observations of the pendulum's motion with the class.	_____

Notes for Home Your child built a pendulum and experimented with its motion.
Home Activity: Ask your child to build a simple pendulum and show one or two ways to change its motion.

Name _____ Date _____

Investigating Force Used to Move Objects

Follow This Procedure

3–5. Record your observations in the chart.

Object	Length of stretched rubber band	
	Smooth surface	**Rough surface**
Empty box		

Interpret Your Results

1. How does the stretch of the rubber band change when you increase the mass of the object?

The stretch of the rubber band increases when the mass

of the object being moved increases.

_____

_____

Make an **inference** to answer the following question: How does the mass of an object affect the force needed to move the object?

Students may infer that objects with greater mass

require more force to move.

_____

_____

2. How did your results change when you used a rough surface?

The stretch of the rubber band increased when the object was moved over a rough surface.

Make an inference to answer the following question: How does the roughness of the surface affect the force needed to make objects move?

Students should infer that more force is needed to move objects across a rough surface.

Inquire Further

How could you reduce the force needed to move the objects? Develop a plan to answer this or other questions you may have.

Students may plan to repeat the activity using surfaces they think are smoother than the surface used in the first part of the activity. Students may also plan to try to wax the surface, or place rollers beneath the box.

Self-Assessment Checklist	
I followed instructions to **measure** the length of a rubber band when moving objects of different masses.	_____
I recorded my **measurements** when moving objects across a smooth surface and a rough surface.	_____
I **compared** the amount of stretch needed to move objects of different masses.	_____
I **described** how my results changed when moving objects across a rough surface.	_____
I made **inferences** about the force needed to move objects of different masses across smooth and rough surfaces.	_____

Notes for Home Your child measured the force needed to move objects of different masses across smooth and rough surfaces.
Home Activity: Ask your child to demonstrate that different amounts of force are needed to move an object across smooth and rough surfaces.

Name _____ Date _____

Investigating Friction

Follow This Procedure

3–5. Record your observations and measurements.

Objects	Observations	Measurements
Eraser		
Stone		
Coin		
Button		
Toy car		

Interpret Your Results

1. Describe some properties of the objects that slide more easily.

Students may note that objects with solid, smooth

surfaces or with wheels slide more easily.

_____

Describe some properties of the objects that slide less easily.

Students may note that objects that have rough

surfaces slide less easily.

_____

Name _____ Date _____

2. Which object demonstrated the most friction with the board? Which demonstrated the least friction?

Objects with rough or soft surfaces demonstrate the most friction; objects with solid, smooth surfaces or movable wheels demonstrate the least friction.

Rank the objects according to how much friction was demonstrated, from most to least. **Answers will vary.**

_____ _____ _____ _____ _____

most   least

Inquire Further

How could you reduce the friction with the board? Develop a plan to answer this or other questions you may have.

Students may plan to place a smooth surface on the board, or a coating to make it smoother.

_____

_____

_____

Self-Assessment Checklist

I followed instructions to demonstrate how friction affects different objects on a wooden ramp.	_____
I recorded my **observations** of the properties of the objects.	_____
I recorded my **measurements** of the board height needed to move each object.	_____
I described properties of objects that affect how the objects slid down a ramp.	_____
I **classified** by ranking the objects according to how much friction was demonstrated.	_____

 Notes for Home Your child **observed** and **measured** the height of a ramp necessary to overcome friction.
Home Activity: Ask your child to identify several objects in your home that would easily slide down a ramp.

Name _____ Date _____

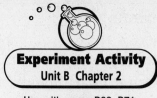
Experimenting with Balloon Rockets

State the Problem

How does the size of a balloon opening affect how far a balloon rocket travels along a string?

Formulate Your Hypothesis

If you make the opening of a balloon smaller, will the distance the balloon rocket travels be reduced? Write your **hypothesis.**

_____

_____

_____

_____

Identify and Control the Variables

The opening of the balloon is the **variable** you can change. The amount of air in each balloon and the size and shape of the balloon must remain the same. You must also release the balloon at the same point each time.

Test Your Hypothesis

1–8. Follow the steps on textbook pages B69–B70 to perform your experiment.

6–7. Record your data in the chart below.

Collect Your Data

Length of blown-up balloon: _____cm

Opening	Opening size	Distance balloon moves
Large	_____ mm	
Medium	_____ mm	
Small	_____ mm	

Name _____ Date _____

Interpret Your Data

Use the data from your chart to make a bar graph.

Balloon Rocket Travel and Opening Size

Distance traveled by balloon rocket (m)

10
9
8
7
6
5
4
3
2
1
0

Large   Medium   Small

Size of opening

State Your Conclusion

How does your hypothesis compare with your results? Explain how the size of the opening affects the distance a balloon rocket can travel.

Large hole allows air to escape before balloon can travel very

far. Small hole does not give enough propulsion to move rocket.

Inquire Further

How far would the balloon rockets travel if the string was held on an incline rather than horizontally? Develop a plan to answer this or other questions you may have.

Answers will vary.

_____

_____

Self-Assessment Checklist	
I made a **hypothesis** about the size of a balloon's opening and the distance it would travel.	_____
I **identified** and **controlled variables** and **experimented** to test my hypothesis.	_____
I **measured** different sizes of balloon openings and the distances the balloons travelled.	_____
I **collected** and **interpreted data** by making a chart and studying a graph.	_____
I **communicated** by stating my conclusion.	_____

 Notes for Home Your child **experimented** to determine how far a balloon rocket will travel.
Home Activity: Ask your child to explain which variables were controlled to complete the experiment.

38 Experiment Activity

Lab Manual

Name _____ Date _____

Modeling Roller Coaster Motion

Explore

4. Make a drawing of the model. Mark on the drawing where you think the marble was speeding up and slowing down.

Students may indicate on their drawings that the marble was speeding up as it moved downhill and slowed down as it moved uphill.

Reflect

1. What did you have to do to the posterboard to make the marble roll all the way over the hill?

    Students should respond that they had to hold the end of the

    posterboard so it was higher than the hill in order to make

    the marble roll all the way over the hill.

2. Make an **inference.** What do you think caused the changes in the marble's speed?

    Students may infer that gravity and friction affected the

    speed of the marble in the model.

Name _____ Date _____

Inquire Further

Can you make the marble roll over two hills? Develop a plan to answer this or other questions you may have.

Students may plan to repeat the activity using two hills

instead of one. Students may need to add an additional piece

of posterboard to the model in order to make a second hill.

_____

_____

_____

_____

_____

_____

Self-Assessment Checklist

I followed instructions to make and use a **model** roller coaster.	_____
I **observed** the movement of the marble on the model roller coaster.	_____
I made a drawing of the model and marked where the marble sped up and slowed down.	_____
I described what I had to do to make the marble roll all the way over the hill.	_____
I made an inference about what caused changes in the marble's speed.	_____

 Notes for Home Your child **made a model** of a roller coaster.
Home Activity: Ask your child to draw a simple roller coaster and explain how the height of the "hills" affects the coaster's ability to reach the end of the track.

Name _____ Date _____

Investigating Potential Energy

Follow This Procedure

5–9. Record your observations in the chart.

Number of textbooks used	Height of ramp	Predicted distance cup will move	Measured distance cup moved
1		X	
2		X	
3			
4			

Interpret Your Results

1. How close were your predictions to your results?

Students should compare their predictions to their results.

What is the relationship between the height of the ramp and the distance the marble moved the cup?

Raising the height of the ramp increases the distance the marble moves the cup.

2. Make **inferences** to answer the following questions: How did raising the height of the ramp affect the potential and kinetic energy of the marble? How did raising the ramp affect the amount of work the marble did?

As the height of the ramp increased, the potential energy of the marble increased and the kinetic energy at the bottom of the ruler increased. The amount of work done increased when the marble was released from a greater height.

Inquire Further

What effect would the mass of the marble have on the distance the cup moves? Develop a plan to answer this or other questions you may have.

Unlike the Explore Activity on page B76, the mass of the marble has an important effect. The greater the mass of the marble, the greater the potential energy. A heavier marble will move the cup farther than a standard marble.

Self-Assessment Checklist	
I followed instructions to **observe** and **measure** the distance a marble can move a cup.	_____
I **collected** and **interpreted data.**	_____
I made **predictions** based on the data.	_____
I stated the relationship between the height of the ramp and the distance the marble moved the cup.	_____
I made **inferences** about the potential and kinetic energy of the marble and the amount of work done by the marble.	_____

Notes for Home Your child **measured** the amount of work done by marbles with different amounts of potential energy.
Home Activity: Ask your child to arrange three identical objects so that they each have a different amount of potential energy.

Investigating Radiant Energy

Follow This Procedure

4–7. Use the chart to record your **observations.** Write an explanation for your **predictions.**

_____

_____

_____

Appearance of paper	Predictions	Observations
Beneath construction paper		**This paper is the lightest.**
Beneath wax paper		**This paper is dark.**
Beneath plastic wrap		**This paper is the darkest.**

Interpret Your Results

1. Which material blocked the most sunlight? Which blocked the least sunlight?

The construction paper blocked the most sunlight.

The plastic wrap blocked the least sunlight.

Explain why there was a difference.

The construction paper is opaque and does not allow sunlight to pass through. The wax paper is translucent and allows some light through. The plastic wrap is transparent and allows light to pass through.

2. What evidence of an energy change did you observe in this activity?

The change in the color of the paper exposed to sunlight indicates a change in energy. The observed color change occurred only after the light-sensitive paper was exposed to radiant light energy from the sun.

Inquire Further

What other materials can be changed by radiant light energy? Develop a plan to answer this or other questions you may have.

Students may mention the effect of radiant energy on vegetables and fruits. Light energy removes Vitamin D from milk in clear or translucent containers. Students may mention how clothing "bleaches" when left in sunlight. Students may mention that light energy makes changes in film in a camera when a picture is taken.

Self-Assessment Checklist	
I followed instructions to test how radiant energy affects light-sensitive paper.	
I recorded my **predictions** and **observations.**	_____
I compared and contrasted the shapes produced on the light-sensitive paper.	_____
I stated which materials blocked the most and the least sunlight.	_____
I stated the evidence of an energy change I observed.	_____

Notes for Home Your child tested the ability of several materials to block radiant energy from the sun from reaching light-sensitive paper.

Home Activity: Ask your child to explain why some products such as vitamins or prescription medicines come in dark packages.

Name _____ Date _____

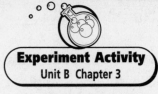
Experimenting with Sunscreens

State the Problem

Are there differences in the effectiveness of sunscreens?

Formulate Your Hypothesis

Do sunscreens with higher SPF values block sunlight better than sunscreens with lower SPF values? Write your **hypothesis.**

_____

_____

Identify and Control the Variables

The SPF value of sunscreen is the **variable** you can change. Remember to keep all other variables—the amount of sunscreen and the length of time in the sun—the same for all the tests.

Test Your Hypothesis

Follow the steps on textbook pages B103–B104 to perform your **experiment.**

Collect Your Data.

Sample	SPF value	Sample of exposed paper	Rank (1 for most effective, to 3 for least effective)
1			
2			
3			
4	no SPF value		no sunscreen

Name _____ Date _____

Interpret Your Data

Classify the samples by ranking them in order from most to least effective.

_____   _____   _____   _____

most effective   least effective

Describe the differences between the sunscreen paper samples and the control paper sample.

The darker the color of the paper, the more sunlight penetrated the sample. Students should classify and rank their samples based on their observations.

State Your Conclusion

How do your results compare with your hypothesis?

_____

Were there great differences, little differences, or no differences among the sunscreen samples?

_____

Inquire Further

Does tanning lotion without sunscreen block sunlight? Develop a plan to answer this or other questions you may have.

Students may plan to repeat the experiment using tanning lotion that does not contain sunscreen.

Self-Assessment Checklist	
I made a **hypothesis** about the effectiveness of sunscreens with different SPF values.	
I **identified** and **controlled variables**.	_____
I followed instructions to perform an **experiment**.	
I **collected** and **interpreted** my **data** by **classifying** paper samples and ranking them from lightest to darkest.	_____
I **communicated** by reporting my conclusion to the class.	_____

Notes for Home Your child **experimented** to find out if sunscreens with higher SPF values block more sunlight.
Home Activity: Ask your child to explain why one strip of transparent tape was tested without sunscreen.

Exploring Electric Charges

Explore

Use with page B110.

3 and 4. Record your observations in the chart below.

Objects tested	Results	
	+ tape	– tape
Ruler rubbed with plastic wrap	repel	attract
Comb rubbed with plastic wrap	repel	attract
Ruler rubbed with wool cloth	attract	repel
Comb rubbed with wool cloth	attract	repel

Reflect

1. Which of the objects attracted the + tape? Which repelled the tape?

Ruler and comb rubbed with wool cloth attracted the

+ tape. Ruler and comb rubbed with plastic wrap repelled

the + tape.

Which of the objects attracted the – tape? Which repelled the tape?

Ruler and comb rubbed with plastic wrap attracted the

– tape. Ruler and comb rubbed with wool cloth repelled

the – tape.

2. Make an **inference.** Describe how charged objects act when brought near other charged objects.

_____

_____

_____

Inquire Further

Do objects without an electric charge attract the charged tape pieces? Develop a plan to answer this or other questions you may have.

Students may plan to repeat the activity using uncharged

objects in place of charged objects.

_____

_____

_____

_____

Self-Assessment Checklist	
I followed instructions to make a charge tester.	_____
I tested objects rubbed with wool and recorded my **observations.**	_____
I tested objects rubbed with plastic wrap and recorded my observations.	_____
I listed objects that attracted and repelled the + tape and the – tape.	_____
I made an **inference** and described how charged objects act when brought near other charged objects.	_____

Notes for Home Your child made two charge testers and observed how the testers reacted when charged objects were brought near them.
Home Activity: Ask your child to explain what happened when charged objects were brought near the charge testers.

Testing Electrical Conductivity

Follow This Procedure

4–7. Record your observations in the chart.

Object	Prediction	Observation
Toothpick	X	**bulb does not light**
Penny	X	**bulb lights up**
Plastic coating on wire	**Students may predict**	**bulb does not light**
Stripped ends of wire	**that metal objects light**	**bulb lights up**
Plastic straw	**the bulb and that**	**bulb does not light**
Paper clip	**nonmetal objects will**	**bulb lights up**
Rubber band	~~not light the bulb.~~	**bulb does not light**
Cardboard strip		**bulb does not light**
Aluminum foil strip		**bulb lights up**

Interpret Your Results

1. Classify each object as a conductor or insulator.

Conductors	Insulators
penny	**toothpick**
stripped ends of wire	**plastic coating on wire**
paper clip	**plastic straw**
aluminum foil strip	**rubber band**
	cardboard strip

What did the objects that were conductors have in common?

All of the conductors were metal.

What did the objects that were insulators have in common?

The insulators were nonmetal.

2. Make an inference. Do you think a gold ring would conduct electricity? Would a piece of wood conduct electricity? Explain.

Students may infer that the gold ring, made of a metal, would conduct electricity; and the wood, not a metal, would not.

3. Make an inference. Why do you think the electrical cords in your home are covered with thick insulation?

Students may infer that the insulator on an electrical cord prevents direct contact with electricity in the conductor inside the wire. This is to prevent dangerous shocks.

Inquire Further

What other objects conduct electricity? Can a liquid be a conductor? Develop a plan to answer these or other questions you may have.

Students may list other metal objects as conductors and other nonmetals as insulators. Some students may know that some acids and saltwater can conduct electricity.

Self-Assessment Checklist	
I followed instructions and used the picture to build a circuit.	_____
I recorded my **predictions**, tested them with the circuit I built, and recorded my **observations.**	_____
I **classified** objects as conductors or insulators.	_____
I made an **inference** about objects that would or would not conduct electricity.	_____
I made an inference about insulation on electrical cords.	_____

Notes for Home Your child built a circuit and tested materials to see if they were electrical conductors or insulators.
Home Activity: Ask your child to identify two electrical conductors and two electrical insulators in your home. Have your child explain his or her choices.

Making a Dimmer Switch

Follow This Procedure

3, 5. Draw the circuit.

6 and 7. Record your observations in the chart.

	Observation of bulb
As wire ends are moved apart	
As wire ends are moved closer together	

Interpret Your Results

1. Describe how the brightness of the bulb changed as you moved the wire ends apart and back together.

The bulb was brightest when two ends of the wire were close

together while touching the graphite and dimmest when the

wires were touching the graphite farther apart.

_____

2. On your drawing, write a B where the wire was placed when the light was brightest. Then write a D where the wire was placed when the light was dimmest.

3. Make an inference. Is graphite a perfect conductor, a perfect insulator, or something in between? Explain.

Students may infer that graphite is neither a perfect conductor nor insulator. As electric current flowed through the increased length of graphite, less electric current flowed.

Inquire Further

What would happen if you used a bare copper wire instead of graphite to make a dimmer switch? Develop a plan to answer this or other questions you may have.

Students may expect that copper wire does not make a good dimmer switch because it is a very good conductor of electricity.

_____

_____

_____

_____

Self-Assessment Checklist

I followed instructions to make a dimmer switch.	_____
I recorded my **observations.**	_____
I described how the brightness of the bulb changed.	_____
I indicated on a drawing where the wire was placed when the bulb was brightest and dimmest.	_____
I made an **inference** about graphite as a conductor and insulator.	_____

Notes for Home Your child built a dimmer switch and made **inferences** about graphite as a conductor.
Home Activity: Ask your child to explain how a dimmer switch works.

Name _____ Date _____

Making a Current Detector

Follow This Procedure

Use with pages B136–B137.

5 and 6. Record your observations in the chart.

	Observations of current detector
Magnet moved inside of coil	
Current detector connected to battery	

Interpret Your Results

1. Why did the needle move when you moved the bar magnet back and forth in the wire coil?

    An electric current passing through the wire creates a

    magnetic field around the wire. This makes the magnetic

    needle of the compass move very slightly.

2. What can you **infer** about current produced by the moving magnet and the current produced by the battery?

    Students may infer that the current produced by the moving

    magnet was much less than the current produced by the

    battery because the needle of the current detector moved

    only slightly when the magnet passed through the coil.

Name _____ Date _____

Inquire Further

What are some ways you could increase the electric current produced by the moving magnet? Develop a plan to answer this or other questions you may have.

Some possible answers are: use a stronger magnet,

increase the number of coils, and move the magnet

faster.

_____

_____

Self-Assessment Checklist

I followed instructions to make a current detector.	_____
I **observed** the current detector when the magnet was moved inside the coil.	_____
I observed the current detector when it was connected to a battery.	_____
I recorded my observations.	_____
I made an **inference** about current produced by the moving magnet and the current produced by the battery.	_____

Notes for Home Your child built a current detector and used it to observe the effects of moving a magnet through a coil of wire.
Home Activity: Ask your child to make a model of the activity using a cardboard tube, string, and a drawing of a compass.

Exploring a Model of the Earth's Layers

Reflect

1. Compare and contrast the different layers. What **observations** can you make about the layers?

Students should note that the innermost layer is the

thickest layer; the crust is extremely thin in comparison to

the other layers.

_____

_____

_____

_____

_____

_____

_____

2. How do you think your model is different from the earth?

The model is much smaller. The earth's real layers are

made of different materials, including solid and melted

rock; the inner layers are under great pressure; the earth's

outer layer, the crust, includes oceans and land masses.

_____

_____

_____

_____

_____

Name _____ Date _____

Inquire Further

How could you change your model to show oceans and land masses of the earth?
Develop a plan to answer this or other questions you may have.

Students may create very thin layers of clay to represent land

masses. These may be added to the outer layer of the model.

The parts not covered by the model land masses may

represent the oceans.

_____

_____

_____

_____

Self-Assessment Checklist	
I followed instructions to make a **model** of the earth.	_____
I **measured** the layers of the model.	_____
I **recorded** observations about my model.	_____
I **compared** the layers of my model.	_____
I compared my model to the earth.	_____

Notes for Home Your child **explored a model** of the earth's layers.
Home Activity: Encourage your child to look for pictures of the earth's layers in magazines or travel brochures, or visit places in your community to see examples of these layers.

Investigating Moving Continents

Follow This Procedure

1–4. Follow the steps on page C12 in your book.

Interpret Your Results

1. How well did your continents fit together? How did you decide to fit them together this way?

Answers will vary. Some students may have based their

arrangements on a combination of the shapes of the

continents and the shaded or colored areas to fit the

continents together.

_____

_____

_____

_____

2. Record the differences and similarities between your map and the world map.

Answers will vary. Students may find different amounts of

detail in the maps. Different types of maps distort

continents in different ways, so students may notice some

variation in size, shape, and proportion of continents.

_____

_____

_____

_____

Name _____ Date _____

3. Do you see any patterns in the colored areas of your continents? If so, what are they?

The colored areas should line up fairly well in noticeable patterns. Students should see how the shapes of the continents and the fossils, coal deposits, glacier deposits, and some mountain ranges often fit together like a puzzle.

_____

_____

Inquire Further

What other ways can the continents fit together? Develop a plan to answer this or other questions you may have.

Students may want to cut out another set of continents to see if there are other ways they could fit them together.

_____

_____

_____

Self-Assessment Checklist	
I followed instructions to **observe** the continent outlines and to **model** how continents may have fit together.	_____
I used different colors to shade in mountains, coal and glacier deposits, and fossils on each continent.	_____
I correctly labeled and cut out the continents, and fit them together.	_____
I **communicated** by discussing similarities and differences between my map and a world map.	_____
I described patterns on my map.	_____

Notes for Home Your child **investigated** how continents fit together.
Home Activity: Using a globe or a map of the world, have your child explain to you how the continents fit together like a puzzle and point out where some fossil and coal deposits are located.

Name _____ Date _____

Investigating Weathering

Follow This Procedure

2–7. Record your **observations** in the chart.

	Observations
Broken chalk	**Some rough edges where chalk is broken**
Chalk after shaking for 5 minutes with stones	**Chalk worn down; edges smooth**
Chalk after placing in vinegar	**Should begin bubbling and breaking down**
Chalk after removing from vinegar	**Chalk may be smaller; edges smoother**

Interpret Your Results

1. Which cup or cups represented physical weathering? Which cup or cups represented chemical weathering?

The cup with stones, water, and chalk represented physical

weathering.

The cup with chalk and vinegar represented chemical

weathering.

_____

_____

_____

_____

2. Was weathering more evident in one cup than the other? Compare and contrast the chalk in the cups.

Results may vary between groups, but most students may note that a similar amount of weathering occurred in the cups. Reduced weathering may occur in the cup with chalk and vinegar if dustless chalk is used.

_____

_____

Inquire Further

How could you change the activity to investigate the combined effects of physical and chemical weathering? Develop a plan to answer this or other questions you may have.

Students could repeat the activity but use the same pieces of chalk for both physical and chemical weathering.

_____

_____

_____

_____

Self-Assessment Checklist	
I followed instructions to **make a model** of weathering.	_____
I recorded my **observations** of the weathering of chalk by water and stones.	_____
I recorded my observations of the weathering of chalk by acid in vinegar.	_____
I identified the weathering of the chalk as physical or chemical weathering.	_____
I compared and contrasted the chalk in the different cups.	_____

Notes for Home Your child **investigated** the effects of physical and chemical weathering on chalk.
Home Activity: Look for signs of weathering on different objects outside (buildings, patio furniture, cars, flower pots, etc.).

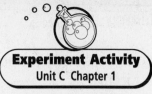

Experimenting with Crystal Formation

State the Problem

How does the rate of cooling affect crystal size?

Formulate Your Hypothesis

When cooling is faster will the size of alum crystals be larger, smaller, or will there be no effect?

_____

_____

Identify and Control the Variables

The rate of cooling the alum solution is the **variable** you can change. Keep the concentration of the solution and the amount of solution the same for each trial.

Test Your Hypothesis

1–9. Follow the steps on textbook pages C35–C36 to perform your experiment.

9. Record your data in the chart below.

Collect Your Data

Observations and measurements of crystals						
Cup	15 min.	30 min.	1 hour	2 hours	4 hours	Measurements
A						
		Data in the charts may vary.				
B						
C						

Interpret Your Data

1. In which cup did crystals form the fastest? the slowest?

Cup B—fastest; Cup C—slowest.

2. In which cup did the smallest crystals form? In which cup did the largest crystals form?

Cup B—smallest; Cup C—largest.

3. Describe how the rate of cooling affects crystal size.

The warmer the water, the slower the cooling, and the larger the crystals that form. Colder water causes rapid cooling and makes crystals form quickly, but the crystals are small.

State Your Conclusion

How did your results compare with your hypothesis? Write a summary of how the rate of cooling affects crystal size.

Students should state that a faster rate of cooling results in smaller crystals; a slower rate results in larger crystals.

Inquire Further

What will happen if you keep the buttons in the solution until the solution evaporates? Develop a plan to answer this or other questions you may have.

Students could keep the buttons in the solution until it has completely evaporated. Crystals should become larger.

Self-Assessment Checklist	
I made a **hypothesis** about the effect the rate of cooling has on the size of crystals that form.	_____
I **identified** and **controlled variables.**	_____
I followed instructions to perform an **experiment** to **observe** crystal formation.	_____
I **collected** and **interpreted data** by **recording observations** and by **measuring** and recording the size of the crystals.	_____
I **communicated** by stating my conclusion about the effect of the rate of cooling on crystal size.	_____

Notes for Home Your child **experimented** to see the effect the rate of cooling has on the size of crystals formed.
Home Activity: Ask your child to explain the results of the experiment to you.

Name _____ Date _____

Exploring the Earth's Resources

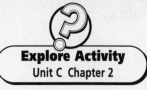
Explore

2. Use the chart to write at least one way that each resource is used by people.

Resources	Uses of Resources

3. Use the chart to classify the objects into categories.

Resources that could be completely used up	
Resources which would be replenished within a human lifetime or less	
Resources which could never be used up	

Reflect

1. How did you decide if a resource could be replenished?

Students may imagine what would happen if the resource continues to be used in the ways it is and then imagine how long it could last. If it won't last forever, they will say it could be used up. Most will consider if resources can grow back or can become pure again.

2. Compare and contrast how different groups made their decisions.

Students should compare and contrast their reasoning as well as their answers.

Inquire Further

Which resources in your classroom or home could be used up? Which could be replenished? Which could never be used up? Develop a plan to answer these or other questions you may have.

Students may plan to list objects in the classroom or in their homes and classify them as they did in this activity.

Self-Assessment Checklist	
I followed instructions to **observe** some of Earth's resources.	_____
I listed uses for the resources.	_____
I listed the resources that could be completely used up, the resources that could be replenished, and the resources that could never be used up.	_____
I recorded the objects that were classified in each group.	_____
I **communicated** by discussing if each resource could be replenished or not.	_____

Notes for Home Your child **explored** Earth's resources.
Home Activity: Discuss with your child the steps your community has taken to protect Earth's resources.

Name _____ Date _____

Investigating
Water Pollution

Follow This Procedure

4–8. Record your observations in the chart.

	Observations
Level of lake water and water under hill	**Students should observe that the level of the water under the hill is the same as the lake level.**
Model before spraying	
Model after 15 minutes	
Model after 30 minutes	**Students should observe that the food coloring has moved down slightly into the sand.**
Model after 1 hour	**Eventually the food coloring spreads through the lake.**
Model after 2 hours	

Interpret Your Results

1. Describe how pollution on land can pollute underground and surface water.

Pollution on land can pollute groundwater and lakes when

rain falls and carries pollution into and over the ground.

_____

_____

_____

Lab Manual

2. Infer what might happen if water could flow down through a landfill into the ground below.

The water may carry pollution from the landfill into the

groundwater and could pollute any nearby water.

3. Compare and contrast your model to a real lake and its surrounding land.

The model shows how pollution can affect groundwater and

surface water. Model contains sand while a real lake would

be surrounded by different soil types. Pollution flows rapidly

in model but would spread more slowly in a real lake.

Inquire Further

How difficult is it to clean the pollution from your model? Develop a plan to answer this or other questions you may have.

Students may plan to rinse the sand with clean water until

the polluted water is clear.

_____

_____

_____

Self-Assessment Checklist	
I followed instructions to **make** and **use** a **model** of underground water pollution.	
I recorded my **observations** about water pollution.	_____
I described how pollution on land can pollute underground and surface water.	_____
⌐w landfills could contribute to water pollution.	_____
contrasted my model to a real lake and its	_____

Investigate Activity

ild **investigated** how pollution on land can pollute underground and surface water.
your child where your household garbage goes and discuss the water sources
e.

Name _____ Date _____

Investigating Air Pollution

Follow This Procedure

Use with pages C68–C69.

5–6. Record your **observations** and data in the chart.

Card Number	Location	Observations
1		
2		
3		
4		

Interpret Your Results

1. Compare and contrast your four cards. Describe the similarities and differences. Which location had the most particles? Which location had the fewest?

   Answers will vary. Cards in similar locations should have similar results. Cards in different locations may differ greatly.

   _____

   _____

   _____

2. Compare and contrast your cards with other groups. Did cards in similar locations show similar results?

   Answers will vary. Cards in similar locations should have similar results.

   _____

   _____

   _____

3. Make an **inference.** Explain why there may be differences in the amount of pollution you observed in different locations.

Particles in the air are one type of pollution. The more particles that are in the air, the more polluted the area. The most polluted area should have the most particles on the detector.

Inquire Further

What are some other ways to detect air pollution? Develop a plan to answer this or other questions you may have.

Students may want to research air pollution or call the EPA to discover what professionals use to study air pollution.

Self-Assessment Checklist	
I followed instructions to make an air pollution detector.	_____
I **observed** the particles on each card and recorded my observations.	_____
I compared and contrasted the cards.	_____
I **communicated** by comparing and contrasting my cards with those of other groups.	_____
I made an **inference** about pollution differences in different locations.	_____

 Notes for Home Your child **made a model** air pollution detector to check pollution levels in different locations.
Home Activity: Ask your child to make predictions about the level of air pollution in different locations within your geographic area.

Name _____ Date _____

Exploring How Sunlight Moves Water

Explore

5. Record your observations in the chart.

	Observations
Day 1 First observation	**Students should observe condensation of water on the underneath of the plastic wrap. Water collects as it slides down the plastic wrap toward the small stone and falls into the cup.**
Second observation	
Third observation	
Day 2 First observation	
Second observation	
Third observation	

Reflect

1. Draw some pictures of what you think happened in the pail. Draw a before-and-after picture.

Students should draw two or more drawings that reflect their observations.

Name _____ Date _____

2. What role did the sunlight play in the pail setup?

The sunlight warmed the water so it evaporated and then

condensed on the bottom surface of the plastic wrap.

_____

_____

Inquire Further

How could you make more water move into the cup in the same amount of time?
Develop a plan to answer this or other questions you may have.

Students may plan to increase the heat by using an

extra lamp or keeping the pail by a heater.

_____

_____

_____

_____

Self-Assessment Checklist	
I followed instructions to make the setup.	_____
I **observed** the pail a few times a day for 1 or 2 days.	_____
I recorded my observations.	_____
I **communicated** by making drawings of what I think happened in the pail.	_____
I described the role of the sunlight in the setup.	_____

Notes for Home Your child **explored** how sunlight moves water through evaporation.
Home Activity: Ask your child to explain how puddles formed on cement when it rains dry up after the sun
comes out.

Name _____ Date _____

Investigating Sunlight and the Earth's Tilt

Follow this Procedure

6–7. Record your observations in the chart.

Tilt of the earth	Part of the Earth receiving more direct sunlight
One-quarter orbit (neither pole tilted toward sun)	
One-half orbit (South Pole tilted toward sun)	
Three-quarters orbit (neither pole tilted toward sun)	
Start/End of orbit (North Pole tilted toward sun)	

Interpret Your Results

1. Explain how the earth's tilt affects how directly light reaches different parts of the earth.

The title of the earth causes the most direct light at the

Northern Hemisphere at the Start/End of the orbit. The

Southern Hemisphere gets the most direct light at the half-

way point of the orbit. At one-quarter and three-quarters, the

tilt causes direct light to reach both hemispheres equally.

_____

_____

Name _____ Date _____

2. Explain the difference in the seasons between the Northern and Southern Hemispheres.

The seasons are opposite for the Northern and Southern Hemispheres. When the North has winter, the South has summer. When the South has fall, the North has spring.

3. Make an inference to answer the question. Which position of the earth would be winter in the Northern Hemisphere? Explain.

Students should infer that the Northern Hemisphere is at the half-way point, or two-quarters, when it is winter.

Inquire Further

How does the length of daylight time at the earth's poles change as the earth orbits the sun? Develop a plan to answer this or other questions you may have.

Students may repeat the seasonal modeling activity and note at which orbit positions the poles are in continuous light or continuous dark.

Self-Assessment Checklist	
I followed instructions to **model** the orbit of the earth.	_____
I **observed** the amount of light on the model.	_____
I recorded my observations.	_____
I explained how the earth's tilt affects how directly light reaches different parts of the earth.	_____
I made an **inference** about the position of the earth when it is winter in the Northern Hemisphere.	_____

Notes for Home Your child **modeled** how sunlight reaches different parts of the earth at different times of the year.
Home Activity: Looking at a globe or world map, discuss what the weather would be like in Australia or New Zealand in December and in June.

Name _____ Date _____

Investigating How a Greenhouse Works

Follow This Procedure

5, 7. Record your measurements in the chart.

	Container without plastic wrap	Container with plastic wrap
Temperature at start		
Temperature at 10 minutes	**Students should note that the covered container is heating up faster than the uncovered one.**	
Temperature at 20 minutes		
Temperature at 30 minutes		

Interpret Your Results

1. How did the temperatures of the two containers compare before they were placed in sunlight?

    Both containers had the same temperature at the start of the activity.

    How did they compare after they were exposed to light for half an hour?

    Both containers got warmer, but the covered container had higher temperatures than the uncovered container.

2. Explain why it is important to use the same amount of soil in each container and to expose them to sunlight for the same amount of time.

    Controlling the variables is important so measurements are not affected by anything other than what is being tested.

3. Based on your measurements, which container do you think was like a greenhouse?

> **The covered container was more like a greenhouse.**

_____

4. Explain how your model is similar to the greenhouse effect on the earth and how it is different.

> **The earth is much larger; contains bodies of water and diverse landforms that affect temperature. The atmosphere is also not a sheet of plastic. Both use sunlight.**

_____

Inquire Further

Would the results be different if you used water in the container instead of soil? Develop a plan to answer this or other questions you may have.

> **Students may wish to repeat the activity using water instead of soil. Variables can be controlled by maintaining the same amount of water and temperature of the water in each container.**

_____

Self-Assessment Checklist	
I followed instructions to **make a model** of a greenhouse.	_____
I recorded my **measurements** of the temperatures of each container every ten minutes.	_____
I compared the air temperatures in the containers before and after they were exposed to sunlight.	_____
I **identified** and **controlled variables** in the activity and discussed why that is important.	_____
I compared my model to the greenhouse effect on the earth.	_____

Notes for Home Your child **made a model** of a greenhouse and investigated how it keeps plants warm.
Home Activity: Ask your child to explain why it is dangerous to leave a pet in a car with the windows rolled up on a sunny day.

Name _____ Date _____

Making a Model of the Solar System

Reflect

Hold the Earth model next to the Venus model, then next to the Jupiter model. Describe how the Earth compares in size to Venus and Jupiter.

Venus is very close in size to Earth. Jupiter is many times

larger than Earth.

_____

_____

_____

_____

_____

_____

_____

Inquire Further

How many Earth models could be lined up along the diameter of the Jupiter model? Develop a plan to answer this or other questions you may have.

Students may use the Earth model to trace a series of

Earth-sized circles across the diameter of Jupiter.

_____

_____

_____

_____

_____

_____

Self-Assessment Checklist	
I followed instructions to make **models** of the planets.	_____
I used the chart to find the correct size for each planet model.	_____
I **measured** each planet drawing to make sure it had the proper diameter.	_____
I **arranged** the planets in order of their position from the sun.	_____
I described how the Earth compares in size to Venus and Jupiter.	_____

Notes for Home Your child **made a model** of the solar system.
Home Activity: With your child, make up a saying to help remember the order and names of the planets.

Name _____ Date _____

Making a Spectroscope

Follow This Procedure

5 and **6.** Record your prediction and observations in the chart.

Prediction	Observations	Drawing
Students should predict that the diffraction grating will separate the light.	Students should observe the visible spectrum and draw it in the right order (red, orange, yellow, green, blue, indigo/violet).	

Interpret Your Results

1. Where have you seen a color pattern like the one in your drawing?

Students may mention a rainbow, a prism, drops of oil, or colors on a bubble's surface.

_____

_____

_____

Name _____   Date _____

2. Explain how the diffraction grating in the spectroscope changes the light from the light bulb.

The diffraction grating bends the light rays to different

degrees, separating the light into its component colors.

_____

_____

_____

Inquire Further

What patterns do other sources of light produce when viewed with the spectroscope? Develop a plan to answer this or other questions you may have.

Different light sources produce different spectrums. Students

may wish to use their spectroscopes to view daylight,

fluorescent light, or other light sources. Caution students to

avoid looking directly at bright light.

_____

Self-Assessment Checklist	
I followed instructions to make a spectroscope.	_____
I **predicted** how light would appear when looking through a spectroscope.	_____
I **observed** light from a bulb through the spectroscope.	_____
I recorded my prediction and observations, and made a drawing.	_____
I explained how the diffraction grating in a spectroscope changes the light from a light bulb.	_____

Notes for Home Your child **made a model** spectroscope to separate white light into the colors of the visible spectrum.
Home Activity: Ask your child to use information from this lesson to speculate about how a rainbow is formed.

Investigating Lenses

Follow This Procedure

2–4 and **6.** Record your observations in the chart.

	Observations
Description of lens shape	**Students should observe that the convex lens is curved outward on both surfaces.**
Drawing of side view of lens	**Their drawing should reflect this.**
Change caused by glass convex lens	**Students should observe that object appears larger, or magnified.**
Change caused by smaller convex lens	**Students should observe objects are magnified more than the first lens.**
Appearance of object through telescope	**Students should observe that objects appear magnified and upside down.**

Interpret Your Results

1. Write an operational definition of a convex lens.

Students' operational definitions may include: A convex lens is thicker in the middle. Objects held close to a convex lens are magnified. Different convex lenses may magnify objects to different degrees.

2. Describe how to make and use a simple refracting telescope.

Students should describe their assembly of the telescope in their own words.

Name _____ Date _____

Describe how to place the lenses and how to focus the telescope.

Place the lens with higher power of magnification near eye; place lens of lower magnification in front of first lens; face a distant object and move the second lens until the object is in focus.

Describe how objects appear when viewed through the telescope.

Object appears magnified and upside down.

_____

_____

_____

Inquire Further

What happens if you use a concave lens as the eyepiece of a simple refracting telescope? Develop a plan to answer these or other questions you may have.

Students may repeat this activity using a concave lens instead of the hand lens as the eyepiece. Students may find different degrees of magnification, and the image is not turned upside-down.

_____

Self-Assessment Checklist	
I followed instructions to record **observations** of objects through convex lenses.	_____
I drew a diagram of a convex lens.	_____
I followed instructions to make and use a simple refracting telescope.	_____
I wrote an **operational definition** of a convex lens.	_____
I described how to make and use a simple refracting telescope.	_____

 Notes for Home Your child **investigated** how convex lenses change the way objects appear.
Home Activity: Challenge your child to think of practical uses for convex lenses in everyday life.

Exploring Lung Volume

Explore

3. **Measure** and record the diameter of the soap ring left on the bag.

_____

_____

Reflect

Make an **inference**. What might account for differences in lung volumes among students?

Students may infer that a person's size or physical fitness level

could affect lung volume. Respiratory disorders, such as

asthma, may also affect lung volume.

_____

_____

Inquire Further

Can regular exercise help you increase your lung volume? Develop a plan to answer this or other questions you may have.

Students may plan a course of regular exercise and repeat the

activity periodically to see if lung volume increases.

_____

_____

_____

_____

Self-Assessment Checklist

I followed instructions to form a bubble dome.   _____

I **measured** the diameter of my bubble after it burst.   _____

I recorded my measurements.   _____

I used information in the table to determine my lung volume.   _____

I **inferred** why there may be differences in lung volume
   among students.   _____

Notes for Home Your child **measured** his or her lung volume by blowing a soap bubble.
Home Activity: Discuss with your child why working to increase lung capacity might be beneficial to a
person's health.

Name _____ Date _____

Making a Breathing Model

Follow This Procedure

5–6. Record your predictions and observations in the chart.

	Predictions	Observations
Balloon pulled down		
Balloon pushed up		

Interpret Your Results

1. How well did your predictions match your observations?

Answers will vary. Students should describe similarities and

differences between their predictions and observations.

_____

2. Compare and contrast the workings of your model with the actual process of breathing. What similarities and differences do you note?

Possible answers: Both the balloon diaphragm and the

human diaphragm help air move in and out of the "lungs."

However, when humans breathe, the diaphragm, which is

curved upward when relaxed, contracts and flattens to pull

air into the chest cavity. The balloon in the model may be

pulled out of a flat shape into a kind of point. Another

difference is that the model does not show the action of the

muscles that pull the ribs up and out for inhaling and that

relax and move the ribs back down and in for exhaling.

_____

3. Make an **inference.** What might be the advantage of having an especially strong diaphragm?

Possible answer: A strong diaphragm can help a person pull more air into the lungs.

Inquire Further

What happens if there is an open hole in the cup? Develop a plan to answer this or other questions you may have.

Students may plan to carefully make a hole or crack in the cup and pull on the balloon diaphragm to see what happens. They should find that there is little or no inflation of the balloon. Similarly, a chest injury that punctures the chest cavity can cause the lungs to fail to inflate.

Self-Assessment Checklist	
I followed instructions to **make a model** of the respiratory system.	_____
I recorded my **predictions** and **observations** about the workings of the model.	_____
I compared my predictions and observations.	_____
I compared and contrasted the model with the actual process of breathing.	_____
I made an **inference** about the advantage of having an especially strong diaphragm.	_____

Notes for Home Your child made a **model** of the respiratory system to show how the diaphragm aids breathing.
Home Activity: Have your child explain what a diaphragm is and how it aids breathing.

Name _____ Date _____

Experimenting with Exercise and Carbon Dioxide

State the Problem

How does the body's activity level affect the amount of carbon dioxide exhaled?

Formulate Your Hypothesis

If you increase your activity level, will the amount of carbon dioxide exhaled increase, decrease, or stay the same? Write your **hypothesis.**

_____

_____

Identify and Control the Variables

Your activity level is the **variable** you can change. Remember to use the same amount of bromothymol blue solution for each trial.

Test Your Hypothesis

1–6. Follow the steps on textbook pages D25–D26 to perform an experiment.

Collect Your Data

Trial	Activity level	Amount of time for color change
1	After resting	
2	After walking	
3	After running	

Interpret Your Data

1. Use the data from your chart to make a bar graph.

Changes in Bromothymol Blue

Time in seconds

220
200
180
160
140
120
100
80
60
40
20
0

Resting   Walking   Running

2. Study your graph. Describe what happened to the amount of time it took for bromothymol blue to turn greenish yellow as the activity level increased.

The bromothymol blue solution changes color in response to the presence of carbon dioxide. As carbon dioxide increases, the color changes more quickly. Blowing into the solution after running changes the color the most quickly.

State Your Conclusion

How do your results compare with your hypothesis? Communicate your results by writing a paragraph. State how exercise affects the amount of carbon dioxide exhaled.

Students should conclude that the amount of carbon dioxide exhaled increases with an increase in activity level.

Inquire Further

Does the amount of carbon dioxide exhaled by people of different heights vary? Develop a plan to answer this or other questions you may have.

Students may plan to repeat the bromothymol blue test with people of different heights as the variable they change.

Self-Assessment Checklist	
I made a **hypothesis** about exercise and exhaling carbon dioxide.	_____
I **identified** and **controlled variables.**	_____
I followed instructions to perform an **experiment.**	_____
I **collected** and **interpreted** my **data** by **recording measurements** and making and studying a graph.	_____
I **communicated** by stating my conclusion.	_____

Notes for Home Your child conducted an **experiment** to see how the body's activity level affects the amount of carbon dioxide exhaled.
Home Activity: Ask your child why it is important to have plenty of fresh air available during physical activity.

Name _____ Date _____

Exploring How Diseases Spread

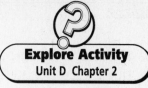

Explore

4. Record your observations in the chart.

	Observations
Sheet 1	
Sheet 2	
Sheet 3	
Sheet 4	

Reflect

1. Describe how shaking hands can spread germs from person to person.

Students may describe how germs may spread from person

to person through direct contact, much as the flour spread

from person to person by shaking hands.

2. Make an **inference.** Besides shaking hands, what are some ways that germs can get on your hands?

Students may infer that germs may be transmitted to hands by coughing or sneezing onto hands, or by touching contaminated objects that others have touched, such as door knobs.

Inquire Further

How can washing your hands affect the spread of germs? Develop a plan to answer this or other questions you may have.

Students may plan to repeat the activity while having one of the students (perhaps the second or third) wash his or her hands before shaking hands with another student. Students should find evidence that washing hands can reduce the spread of germs from person to person.

Self-Assessment Checklist	
I followed instructions to model how some diseases can be spread.	_____
I **observed** handprints left on the four pieces of construction paper.	_____
I recorded my **observations.**	_____
I described how shaking hands can spread germs from person to person.	_____
I made an **inference** about ways that germs can get on hands.	_____

Notes for Home Your child **modeled** how some diseases can be spread from person to person by shaking hands.
Home Activity: Ask your child why it is important to wash hands with antibacterial soap.

Measuring Heart Rates

Follow This Procedure

3–4. Record your measurements in the chart.

Activity	Heartbeats in 10 seconds	Number of heartbeats per minute
Resting heart rate		
Exercising heart rate		

Interpret Your Results

1. Describe how your heart rate changed after exercise.

Students should experience higher (faster) heart rates after exercise, but specific resting and after-exercise heart rates may vary from student to student.

2. Make an **inference.** Why do you think your heart rate changed in this way?

Students may infer that heart rates increase during exercise because body cells need more oxygen and nutrients and produce more wastes than when the body is at rest. The heart beats faster to pump more blood to body cells, to deliver oxygen and nutrients, and to carry away wastes.

3. What are some possible reasons for the variations in resting heart rates and exercising heart rates among your classmates?

Students have learned that a heart strengthened by exercise pumps more blood with each beat, so they should realize that a reason for different heart rates is the level of the cardiovascular (heart) fitness. People who exercise regularly generally have lower heart rates, both while resting and while exercising, than do people who do not exercise.

Inquire Further

If you continue doing jumping jacks, how will your heart rate change? Develop a plan to answer this or other questions you may have.

Students may plan to repeat the activity while extending the amount of time in exercise. Students should observe the same safety precautions as in the activity.

Self-Assessment Checklist	
I followed instructions to **measure** my resting heart rate and my exercising heart rate.	_____
I **collected data** by recording **measurements** in a chart.	_____
I described how my heart rate changed after exercise.	_____
I made an **inference** about why my heart rate changed when I exercised.	_____
I **communicated** by discussing possible reasons for variations in resting heart rates and exercising heart rates.	_____

Notes for Home Your child **measured** his or her resting heart rate and exercising heart rate.
Home Activity: Have your child show you how to find your resting heart rate and then compare his or her resting heart rate to yours.

Contents   Part 2: Performance-Based Assessment

UNIT A   LIFE SCIENCE

Activity Preview: You will imagine that you and your partner have entered the local Science Fair. Your task is to place samples representing living and nonliving things on a poster along with samples of producers, consumers, and decomposers.

UNIT B   PHYSICAL SCIENCE

Activity Preview: You will imagine that you work in a science and energy museum. You have been asked to complete the information on the tags for an exhibit on potential and kinetic energy. The tags describe the types of energy in the exhibits.

UNIT C   EARTH SCIENCE

Activity Preview: You will imagine that you are an apprentice in an architecture office. The head architect asks you to select the best material to be used on the outside of a building for the entrance, front walkway, and front stairs.

UNIT D   THE HUMAN BODY

Activity Preview: You will imagine that you and your partner have
                      delayed turning in your science lab reports until the
                      last minute. Your partner has graphed the results, but
                      her computer crashed before she could label the
                      graphs. Now you have to accurately label the graphs.

Materials List

Station 1

Consumable

Nonconsumable

1 hand lens

1 slide containing celery cells

1 slide containing salt grains

1 microscope

Station 2

Consumable

Nonconsumable

1 hand lens

1 slide containing animal cells

1 slide containing chalk slice

1 microscope

Station 3

Consumable

Nonconsumable

1 hand lens

1 slide containing mushroom or yeast cells

1 slide containing mica slice

1 microscope

Additional materials to set up the Stations

How to Set Up

Station 1

Materials

1 hand lens
1 slide containing celery cells
1 slide containing salt grains
1 microscope

Preparation

1. Use a grease pencil or china marker to label the celery slide "A" and the salt slide "B."
2. Students will use a hand lens or microscope to compare the celery cells and salt grains.

Helpful Information

- Students should be able to see the vascular structure of the celery cells with the hand lens.
- Students can use the microscope to see the cell structure of celery.
- Students should determine that sample A is living plant material because it has cell walls and chloroplasts.
- Students can use either the hand lens or the microscope to observe the characteristic crystal structure of the salt grains.
- Students should determine that sample B is nonliving.

Setup

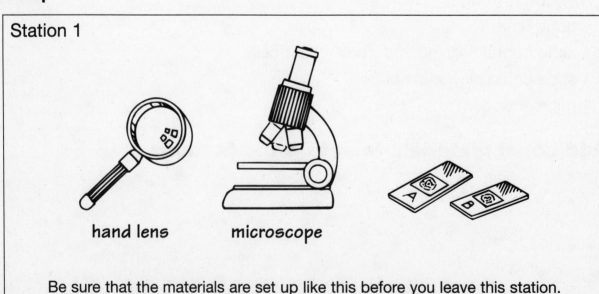

Station 1

hand lens   microscope

Be sure that the materials are set up like this before you leave this station.

How to Set Up

Station 2

Materials

1 hand lens

1 slide containing animal cells

1 slide containing chalk slice

1 microscope

Preparation

1. Use a grease pencil or china marker to label the chalk slide "C" and the animal slide "D."

2. Students will use a hand lens or microscope to compare the chalk slice and animal cells.

Helpful Information

- Students can use the microscope to see the cell structure of the animal sample.

- Students should determine that sample D is living animal material because each cell has a membrane, nucleus, and cytoplasm.

- Students can use either the hand lens or the microscope to observe the characteristics of the chalk.

- Students should determine that sample C is nonliving.

Setup

Station 2

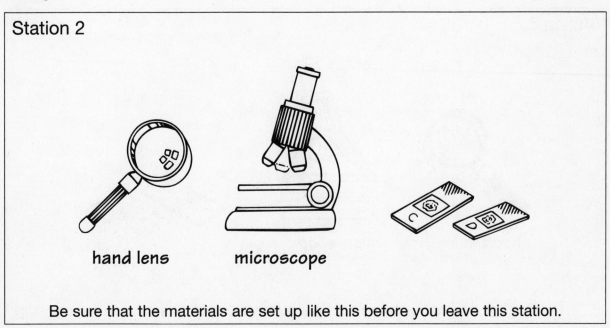

hand lens   microscope

Be sure that the materials are set up like this before you leave this station.

How to Set Up

Station 3

Materials

1 hand lens

1 slide containing mushroom or yeast cells

1 slide containing mica slice

1 microscope

Preparation

1. Use a grease pencil or china marker to label the mica slide "E" and the mushroom or yeast slide "F."

2. Students will use a hand lens or microscope to compare the mica slice and mushroom or yeast cells.

Helpful Information

- Students can use the microscope to see the cell structure of the mushroom or yeast.

- Students should determine that sample F is living material because it has cell walls.

- Students can use either the hand lens or the microscope to observe the characteristics of the mica.

- Students should determine that sample E is nonliving.

Setup

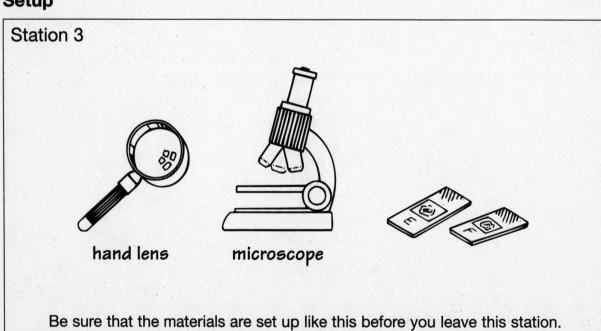

Station 3

hand lens   microscope

Be sure that the materials are set up like this before you leave this station.

Evaluation Guide

Station 1

Purpose

To evaluate a student's ability to compare living and nonliving samples and to identify cell structures such as cell wall, vascular system, and chloroplast.

Criteria

3 points = Student identifies the cell wall, vascular system, and chloroplast of the celery cells.

2 points = Student draws cells without identifying cell structures.

1 point = Student does not draw observations of either sample.

Station 2

Purpose

To evaluate a student's ability to compare living and nonliving samples and to identify cell structures such as cell membrane, nucleus, and cytoplasm.

Criteria

3 points = Student identifies cell membrane, nucleus, and cytoplasm.

2 points = Student draws cells without identifying structures.

1 point = Student does not draw observations of either sample.

Station 3

Purpose

To evaluate a student's ability to compare living and nonliving samples and to identify cell structures such as cell wall.

Criteria

3 points = Student identifies cell wall.

2 points = Student draws cells without identifying structures.

1 point = Student does not draw observations of either sample.

Data Analysis

Purpose

To evaluate a student's ability to distinguish between living and nonliving things, and to classify living things as either producers (those with chloroplasts), consumers (those with cell membranes), or decomposers (those without chloroplasts or cell membranes).

Answers to sample placement:

	Exhibit 1 Producer	Exhibit 2 Consumer	Exhibit 3 Decomposer	Exhibit 4 Nonliving
Slide Sample	A	D	F	B, C, E

Criteria

3 points = Student accurately distinguished nonliving things and identified samples as either producer, consumer, or decomposer.

2 points = Student accurately identified nonliving and living samples and accurately identified either plant or animal cells.

1 point = Student did not distinguish living and nonliving samples.

Performance Activity Scoring Guide

Points	% equivalent
12	100
11	92
10	83
9	75
8	67
7	58
6	50
5	42
4	33
3	25
2	16
1	8

Imagine that you and your partner have entered the local Science Fair. Your entry focuses on living and nonliving things. Your task is to place samples representing living and nonliving things on a poster. You must also place samples of producers, consumers, and decomposers. Make observations of samples A, B, C, D, E, and F and then decide which sample belongs where on the poster.

My Data Collection

Station 1

Use the card at the station to correctly set up the equipment.

Exhibit 1

Look at samples A and B closely. Use the hand lens alone or the hand lens and the microscope. Draw a sketch of what you observe. Label any of the following structures you see: *cell membrane, cell wall, nucleus, cytoplasm, vascular system, and chloroplast.*

Station 2

Use the card at the station to correctly set up the equipment.

Exhibit 2

Look at samples C and D closely. Use the hand lens alone or the hand lens and the microscope. Draw a sketch of what you observe. Label any of the following structures you see: *cell membrane, cell wall, nucleus, cytoplasm, vascular system, and chloroplast.*

Station 3

Use the card at the station to correctly set up the equipment.

Exhibit 3

Look at samples C and D closely. Use the hand lens alone or the hand lens and the microscope. Draw a sketch of what you observe. Label any of the following structures you see: *cell membrane, cell wall, nucleus, cytoplasm, vascular system, and chloroplast.*

My Data Analysis

Now you have taken a close look at all the samples. Use your observations and what you know about living things to decide where to place each sample on the poster. Explain your choices.

	Exhibit 1 Producer	Exhibit 2 Consumer	Exhibit 3 Decomposer	Exhibit 4 Nonliving
Slide Sample				

_____

_____

_____

_____

_____

_____

Materials List

Station 1

Consumable

Nonconsumable

1 flashlight without batteries

1 flashlight with 2 D batteries in place

Station 2

Consumable

Nonconsumable

metric ruler

flashlight with 2 D batteries

radiometer

Station 3

Consumable

Nonconsumable

2 flashlights without batteries

stack of 6 textbooks

board (one meter long)

paper drinking cup

Additional materials to set up the Stations

masking tape (Stations 2 and 3)

How to Set Up

Station 1

Materials

1 flashlight without batteries, labeled "A"

1 flashlight with 2 D batteries in place, labeled "B"

Preparation

1. Because students will be asked to compare the two flashlights, the flashlights need to be labeled. Label the flashlight without batteries "A"; label the flashlight with batteries "B." Be certain flashlight B has two batteries and works.

2. Direct students to turn off the flashlights when they are not in use.

Helpful Information

- When a flashlight lights, the (stored) chemical energy in the batteries is changed to electrical energy and then to light energy.

- Allow students to open flashlights to determine why one does not light.

- Students should note that no energy changes are taking place in the flashlight without an energy source.

Setup

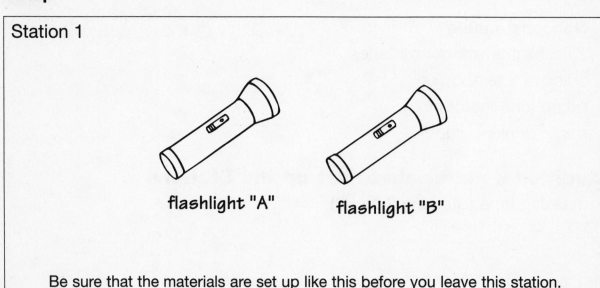

Station 1

flashlight "A"   flashlight "B"

Be sure that the materials are set up like this before you leave this station.

How to Set Up

Station 2

Materials

radiometer

metric ruler

flashlight with 2 D batteries

masking tape

Preparation

1. Make certain that the flashlight is working and that the batteries have not worn out.

2. Use masking tape to secure the base of the radiometer to the table so that it will not accidentally fall and break.

3. Direct students to turn off the flashlight when it is not in use.

Helpful Information

• Radiant energy from the flashlight reaches the vanes, heating them. The black sides of the vanes absorb more energy than the silver sides, causing the vanes to spin.

• Students should realize that the radiant energy from the flashlight somehow moves the vanes, therefore the radiant energy does work.

• The closer the light is to the radiometer, the faster the vanes spin.

Setup

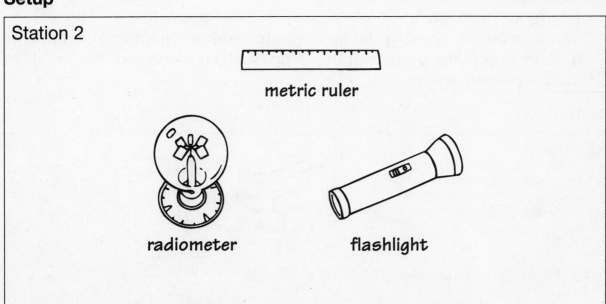

Station 2

metric ruler

radiometer   flashlight

Be sure that the materials are set up like this before you leave this station.

How to Set Up

Station 3

Materials

2 flashlights without batteries, label one "C" and the other "D"

stack of 6 textbooks

paper drinking cup

board (one meter long)

masking tape

Preparation

1. Because students will be asked to compare flashlights, label one flashlight "C" and the other "D."

2. Make certain the batteries have been removed from each flashlight.

3. Place flashlight C on top of the stack of books. Use the board to make a ramp from the top of the books to the table top. Use tape to secure the board to the table top.

4. Place flashlight D on the table top.

Helpful Information

- Allow students to inspect the inside of each flashlight.

- Potential energy is the energy of position. Flashlight C, on top of the stack of books, has more potential energy than the flashlight resting on the table top.

- Energy is the ability to do work. Students can show that flashlight C can do work by allowing the flashlight to slide down a ramp and move a paper cup at the bottom of the ramp. While it is moving, the flashlight exhibits kinetic energy.

Setup

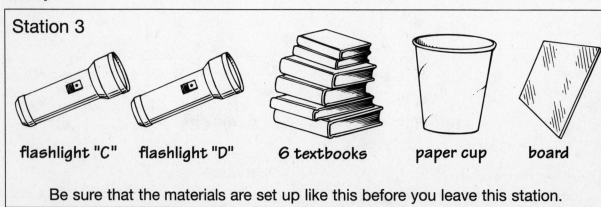

Station 3

flashlight "C"   flashlight "D"   6 textbooks   paper cup   board

Be sure that the materials are set up like this before you leave this station.

Evaluation Guide

Station 1

Purpose

To evaluate a student's ability to identify which flashlight has more stored, or potential, energy and to identify the source of that energy.

Criteria

3 points = Student identified the flashlight with stored, or potential, energy and the source of the energy.

2 points = Student described what happened in one of the flashlights.

1 point = Student did not describe what happened in either flashlight.

Station 2

Purpose

To evaluate a student's ability to recognize radiant energy and kinetic energy and to describe how distance from the radiometer affects the speed of the vanes.

Criteria

3 points = Student identified radiant and kinetic energy and recorded observations using a radiometer.

2 points = Student observed the flashlight's effect on the radiometer.

1 point = Student did not record any observations.

Station 3

Purpose

To evaluate a student's ability to identify which flashlight has more potential energy, to show that the energy can do work, and to identify any kinetic energy observed.

Criteria

3 points = Student identified the flashlight with more potential energy, showed that the flashlight can do work, and identified kinetic energy.

2 points = Student identified the flashlight with more stored, or potential, energy.

1 point = Student did not record any observations.

Data Analysis

Purpose

To evaluate a student's ability to identify and describe any potential and kinetic energy in each of the three exhibits.

Answers to the exhibit tags

Tag 1: B; the flashlight with batteries and a complete circuit has chemical energy stored in its battery.

Tag 2: radiant; vanes turn; faster; kinetic

Tag 3: C; C; do work; C; it slides down the ramp

Criteria

3 points = Student accurately described the energy in all three exhibits.

2 points = Student accurately described the energy in one or two exhibits.

1 point = Student did not describe the energy in any of the exhibits.

Performance Activity Scoring Guide

Points	% equivalent
12	100
11	92
10	83
9	75
8	67
7	58
6	50
5	42
4	33
3	25
2	16
1	8

Imagine that you work in a science and energy museum. You've been asked to complete the information on the tags for an exhibit on potential and kinetic energy. The tags describe the types of energy in the exhibits.

My Data Collection

Station 1

Use the card at the station to correctly set up the equipment.

Exhibit 1

Turn on both flashlights. Observe what happens.

- Compare the energy changes, if any, you observe.

_____

_____

_____

_____

_____

_____

Station 2

Use the card at the station to correctly set up the equipment.

Exhibit 2

Shine the flashlight on the radiometer. Identify any type or kind of energy you observe. Describe how the speed of the vanes changes when the light is at different distances.

- Record your observations.

_____

_____

_____

_____

_____

_____

Station 3

Use the card at the station to correctly set up the equipment.

Exhibit 3

Turn on both flashlights. Observe what happens. Use the materials on the table to show that one of the flashlights has more potential energy than the other.

• Describe how you were able to show that one flashlight had more potential energy and could do work.

_____

_____

_____

• Describe any observations you make about kinetic energy.

_____

_____

_____

My Data Analysis   Answers appear on page 92F.

Now that you have tested each part of the exhibit, use the data you have collected and what you know about energy to complete the following exhibit tags by filling in the blanks.

Exhibit 1 Tag

Flashlight _____ has more stored, or potential, energy. The flashlights have different amounts of potential energy because

_____.

Exhibit 2 Tag

The _____ energy from the flashlight did work by making the _____. The vanes turned _____ when the flashlight was close to the radiometer. The turning vanes are an example of _____ energy.

Exhibit 3 Tag

Flashlight _____ has more stored, or potential, energy. You can show that flashlight _____ has potential energy by showing that it can _____. Flashlight _____ has kinetic energy while _____.

Materials List

Station 1

Consumable

Nonconsumable

1 mineral sample: calcite

1 mineral sample: talc

1 hand lens

1 metric ruler

Station 2

Consumable

Nonconsumable

1 rock sample: quartz

1 rock sample: granite

1 hand lens

1 metric ruler

Station 3

Consumable

Nonconsumable

1 mineral sample: calcite

1 mineral sample: talc

1 mineral sample: quartz

1 rock sample: granite

1 steel nail

Additional materials to set up the Stations

How to Set Up

Station 1

Materials

1 calcite sample
1 talc sample
hand lens
metric ruler

Preparation

1. Label calcite sample "A" and talc sample "B."
2. Students will use a metric ruler and a hand lens to compare the color, luster, and breakage pattern of calcite and talc.
3. You may need to break the sample with a hammer so students can observe breakage pattern.

Helpful Information

- The color of calcite and talc varies from one sample to another because of impurities in the minerals.
- Students should be able to identify the greasy luster of talc (also called soapstone) and the glassy luster of calcite.
- Talc breaks in sheets or layers. Calcite breaks result in small rectangular pieces.

Setup

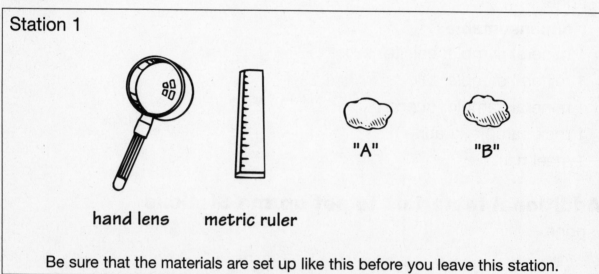

Station 1

hand lens   metric ruler   "A"   "B"

Be sure that the materials are set up like this before you leave this station.

How to Set Up

Station 2

Materials

1 quartz sample

1 granite sample

hand lens

metric ruler

Preparation

1. Label quartz sample "C" and granite sample "D."

2. Students will use a metric ruler and a hand lens to compare the color, luster, and breakage pattern of quartz and granite.

3. You may need to break the sample with a hammer so students can observe breakage pattern.

Helpful Information

• Quartz is a one-mineral sample. Granite is composed of a number of minerals—mostly quartz, feldspar, and biotite.

• Quartz has a glassy luster. Students may be able to identify the quartz crystals in granite.

• Quartz breaks into circular patterns.

Setup

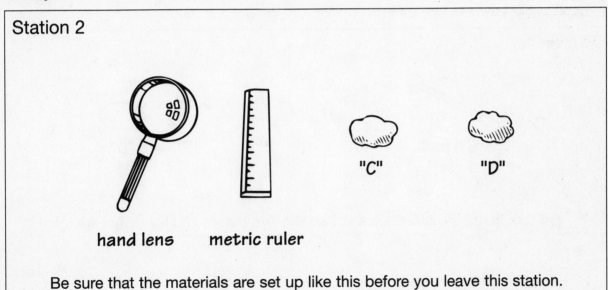

Station 2

hand lens   metric ruler   "C"   "D"

Be sure that the materials are set up like this before you leave this station.

How to Set Up

Station 3

Materials

  1 calcite sample

  1 talc sample

  1 quartz sample

  1 granite sample

  1 steel nail

Preparation

1. Students will use their fingernails (hardness: 2) and a steel nail (hardness: 5) to determine the relative hardness of talc, calcite, and quartz.

2. Label the samples.

Helpful Information

* On the Moh's scale of hardness, the minerals are talc (hardness: 1), calcite (hardness: 3), quartz (hardness: 7). Students do not need to test granite.

* A fingernail can scratch talc; the steel nail can scratch both talc and calcite. Students should show that the minerals from softest to hardest are talc (B), calcite (A), and quartz (C).

Setup

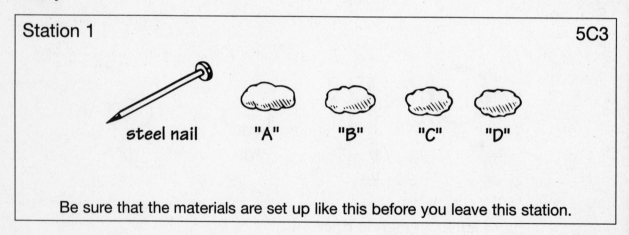

Station 1   5C3

steel nail   "A"   "B"   "C"   "D"

Be sure that the materials are set up like this before you leave this station.

Evaluation Guide

Station 1

Purpose

To evaluate a student's ability to compare talc and calcite with respect to color, luster, and breakage pattern.

Criteria

3 points = Student recorded comparisons of all three of the properties listed.

2 points = Student recorded comparisons of one of the properties listed.

1 point = Student recorded no observations.

Station 2

Purpose

To evaluate a student's ability to compare quartz and granite with respect to color, luster, and breakage pattern.

Criteria

3 points = Student recorded comparisons of all three of the properties listed.

2 points = Student recorded comparisons of one of the properties listed.

1 point = Student recorded no observations.

Station 3

Purpose

To evaluate a student's ability to determine the relative hardness of three minerals.

Criteria

3 points = Student recorded ten or more correct answers.

2 points = Student recorded five or more correct answers.

1 point = Student recorded no correct answers.

	A	B	C	D
One mineral in the sample?	yes	yes	yes	no
Scratched by fingernail?	no	yes	no	n/a
Scratched by steel nail?	yes	yes	no	n/a
Arrange the three single minerals from softest (1) to hardest (3).	2	1	3	

Data Analysis

Purpose

To evaluate a student's ability to identify desirable properties for construction materials, such as a material's hardness, sparkle, luster, breakage pattern, and so on.

Criteria

3 points = Student made a selection supported by two or more desirable properties.

2 points = Student made a suggestion supported by one desirable property.

1 point = Student did not make a suggestion or made a suggestion but provided no supporting properties.

Performance Activity Scoring Guide

Points	% equivalent	Points	% equivalent
12	100	6	50
11	92	5	42
10	83	4	33
9	75	3	25
8	67	2	16
7	58	1	8

Suppose that you are an apprentice in an architecture office. The head architect asks you to select the best material for the outside of a new building. The material will be used for the entrance, front walkway, and front stairs of a public building. Consider the properties of samples A, B, C, and D as you make a recommendation for the material.

My Data Collection

Station 1

Use the card at the station to correctly set up the equipment.

Material Test 1

Look closely at the samples labeled A and B. Use the ruler and the hand lens to observe the samples and compare their color, luster, and breakage pattern.

- Record your observations.

_____

_____

_____

_____

_____

_____

Station 2

Use the card at the station to correctly set up the equipment.

Material Test 1

Look closely at the samples labeled C and D. Use the ruler and the hand lens to observe the samples and compare their color, luster, and breakage pattern.

- Record your observations.

_____

_____

_____

_____

_____

Station 3

Use the card at the station to correctly set up the equipment.

Exhibit 3

Decide which sample is made up of more than one mineral. Use your fingernail and a steel nail to test the hardness of samples that are made up of only one mineral.

Use your observations to complete the table. Answer *yes* or *no*.

	A	B	C	D
One mineral in the sample?				
Scratched by fingernail?				
Scratched by steel nail?				
Arrange the three single minerals from softest (1) to hardest (3).				

My Data Analysis

Now you have completed the materials tests. Use the data you've collected and what you know about rocks, minerals, and physical weathering to make a suggestion for materials to use in a building.

Select the sample you would suggest to use for the entrance way, front walkway, and stairs of a public building. Explain your choice.

_____

_____

_____

_____

Materials List

Station 1

Consumable

Nonconsumable

stopwatch or second timer

jump rope

Station 2

Consumable

Nonconsumable

stopwatch or second timer

tennis ball or other soft rubber ball

Station 3

Consumable

Nonconsumable

200 math counters or pennies

Additional materials to set up the Stations

How to Set Up

Station 1
Materials
stopwatch or second timer

jump rope

illustration showing how to take a pulse

Preparation
1. Demonstrate to students how to take a pulse.
2. Students will use a timer and a jump rope to compare their heart rates at rest and after exercise.

Helpful Information
- When extra exertion requires that more oxygen reach the body's tissues, the speed at which the heart pumps increases. The increases are brought about by nerve impulses and production of certain hormones.
- Make certain that no student has a medical condition that precludes them from several minutes of moderate exercise.

Setup

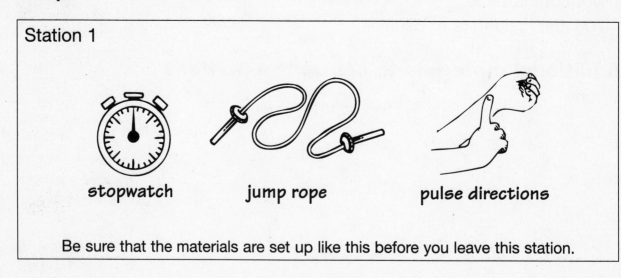

Station 1

stopwatch   jump rope   pulse directions

Be sure that the materials are set up like this before you leave this station.

How to Set Up

Station 2

Materials

stopwatch or second timer

tennis ball or other soft rubber ball

Preparation

1. Students will use a stopwatch and a rubber ball to measure muscle fatigue.

Helpful Information

• As the time of an exercise increases, the muscles involved may not get enough oxygen and may become fatigued. As a result, performance is decreased.

Setup

Station 2

stopwatch

rubber ball

Be sure that the materials are set up like this before you leave this station.

How to Set Up

Station 3

Materials

200 math counters or pennies

Preparation

1. Students will use counters or pennies to model the number of virus cells after each cell has divided 5 times.

Helpful Information

- One of the concerns with the spread of disease is the rate at which disease cells can duplicate. This model shows how quickly 1 cell can divide to form 127 cells.

Setup

Station 3

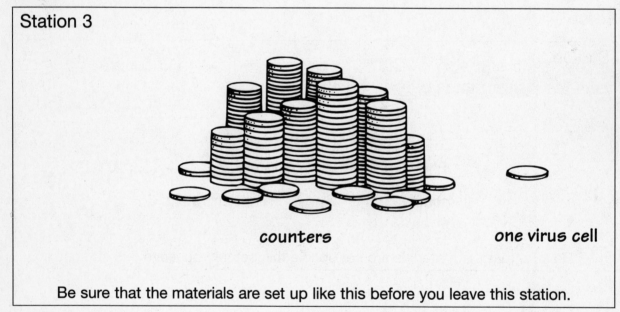

counters   one virus cell

Be sure that the materials are set up like this before you leave this station.

Evaluation Guide

Station 1

Purpose

To evaluate a student's ability to identify that heart rate increases with exercise.

Criteria

3 points = Student records heart rates taken at rest and after 4 intervals of activity and concludes that they increase with exercise.

2 points = Student records heart rates but does not identify that heart rate increases with exercise.

1 point = Student does not record heart rates accurately and does not identify that heart rate increases with exercise.

Station 2

Purpose

To evaluate a student's ability to recognize that muscle fatigue can decrease performance over time.

Criteria

3 points = Student records performance levels after regular time intervals and recognizes that muscle fatigue decreases performance.

2 points = Student records performance levels.

1 point = Student does not record any observations or recognize the connection between muscle fatigue and decreased performance.

Station 3

Purpose

To evaluate a student's ability to model the growth of a virus.

Criteria

3 points = Student accurately models cell division and accurately calculates the resulting number of cells.

2 points = Student models cell division but is unable to calculate the resulting number of cells.

1 point = Student is unable to model cell division and calculate the resulting number of cells.

Data Analysis

Purpose

To evaluate a student's ability to describe the relationship between specific variables and to identify the graphs that represent the relationships.

Sample titles for graphs

Graph A: Heart Rate Increases with Exercise

Graph B: Performance Decreases with Continued Exercise

Graph C: Virus Cells Multiply Quickly

Criteria

3 points = Student accurately describes all three graphs.

2 points = Student accurately describes one of the graphs.

1 point = Student does not describe any of the graphs.

Performance Activity Scoring Guide

Points	% equivalent
12	100
11	92
10	83
9	75
8	67
7	58
6	50
5	42
4	33
3	25
2	16
1	8

Imagine that you and your partner have delayed turning in your science lab reports until the last minute. Your partner has graphed the results, but her computer crashed before she could label the graphs. Use the results of the following activities to accurately label the graphs.

My Data Collection

Station 1

Use the card at the station to correctly set up the equipment.

Activity 1

Follow the directions in the illustration to take your pulse as you sit quietly at the lab table. Then jump rope for 25 rope turns and take your pulse a second time. Resume jumping rope, taking your pulse three more times— at 50, 75, and 100 rope turns.

• Record your observations.

_____

_____

_____

_____

_____

Station 2

Use the card at the station to correctly set up the equipment.

Activity 2

Squeeze the rubber ball as quickly as you can. Count the number of squeezes you can complete in 30 seconds. Continue squeezing the ball for two more minutes, counting the number of squeezes each 30 seconds.

• Record your observations.

_____

_____

_____

_____

_____

Station 3

Use the card at the station to correctly set up the equipment.

Activity 3

Use the counters to make a model of the growth of a virus. Place one counter by itself. Then use counters to show how many cells exist after the first cell divides in two. Next show how many cells there are after each of those cells divides in two. Continue until you have modeled 5 cell divisions.

• Draw a picture of your model.

My Data Analysis

Now you have completed each of the activities. Use the data you've collected to correctly describe each of the following graphs.

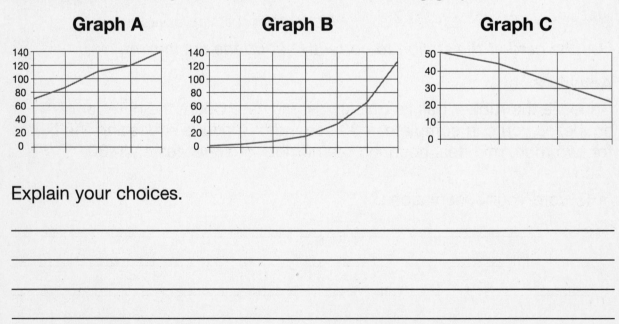

| Graph A | Graph B | Graph C |

Explain your choices.

_____

_____

_____

_____

Contents   Part 3: Science Process Skills

SKILL 7: MAKING OPERATIONAL DEFINITIONS

Skill Preview: An operational definition is a statement of specific information about an object or a phenomenon based on experience. Operational definitions are precise and, in some cases, based on mathematical relationships.

SKILL 8: MAKING AND USING MODELS

Skill Preview: Scientists develop models on the basis of acceptable hypotheses that have yet to be tested. Models may be either physical or mental representations to explain an idea, object, or event.

SKILL 9: FORMULATING QUESTIONS AND HYPOTHESES

Skill Preview: Questions are problems to be solved through application of the other inquiry/process skills. The skill of hypothesizing consists of devising a statement that can be tested by experiment.

SKILL 10: COLLECTING AND INTERPRETING DATA

Skill Preview: Collecting data involves gathering information about observations and measurements in a systematic way and recording that data. It may also involve designing data-gathering procedures.

SKILL 11: IDENTIFYING AND CONTROLLING VARIABLES

Skill Preview: Identifying and controlling variables involves identifying factors that may affect the outcome of an event, or that are not part of the hypothesis being tested. This skill also involves manipulating one factor while other factors are held constant.

SKILL 12: EXPERIMENTING

Skill Preview: Experimenting involves drawing conclusions based on the results of an investigation designed to test a hypothesis or solve a problem. Experimenting is a complex skill combining the other process skills.

Lab Manual

Practice Observing

Follow This Procedure

1–7. Record your observations and drawings in the chart.

	Observations of leaves on three trees	Other observations about the three trees	How many trees on the way to school?
Day 1			
Day 2			

Thinking About Your Thinking

Which observations did you most refine through repetition?

_____

_____

_____

_____

_____

_____

_____

_____

_____

_____

Compare notes with your classmates. Did they improve their observations by repeating them? Which ones did they most refine?

_____

_____

_____

_____

_____

_____

_____

_____

_____

Self-Assessment Checklist	
I made careful **observations** using my senses.	_____
I recorded my observations.	_____
I refined my observations by observing the trees a second time.	_____

 Notes for Home Your child used several senses to observe trees.
Home Activity: Have your child make observations of a piece of furniture in your home. Then have your child repeat and refine those observations.

Name _____ Date _____

Practice Communicating

Follow This Procedure

1–4. Record your descriptions of the rocks in the chart.

Rock	Description

How many types of rocks did you observe?

_____

Describe the rocks by their size, color, and hardness.

_____

_____

_____

_____

5. Describe how the rocks vary. Describe similarities and differences.

_____

_____

_____

_____

6. Make a chart of the qualities of your rocks.

Thinking About Your Thinking

Compare your chart to those of your classmates. How were they alike and different?

_____

_____

_____

How would the rocks be different in an environment unlike the one you live in? Why do you think this is so?

_____

_____

_____

Self-Assessment Checklist	
I **observed** rocks and described them by various qualities.	_____
I recorded my descriptions in a chart.	_____
I made a graph of the qualities listed in my chart.	_____
I **compared** my graph to those of my classmates.	_____

Notes for Home Your child observed rocks and wrote descriptions distinguishing one from another. *Home Activity:* Have your child choose three pieces of furniture in your home and describe each by their various qualities, similarities, and differences.

Practice Classifying

Process Skill Activity

Follow This Procedure

Use with page 11.

1–5. Record your data in the chart.

Name	Quartz	Pyrite	Graphite
Color			
Streak			
Luster			
Hardness			

Thinking About Your Thinking

Do any of these minerals have the same characteristics?

_____

_____

_____

_____

_____

_____

_____

_____

_____

Name _____ Date _____

What uses do you think these minerals might have? Use your classification chart to help you answer this question.

_____

_____

_____

_____

_____

_____

_____

Self-Assessment Checklist

I **classified** minerals according to several different characteristics.	_____
I used the information in my classification chart to determine how the minerals are alike and different.	_____
I made **inferences** about what uses the minerals might have.	_____

Notes for Home Your child classified minerals according to different characteristics to discover their similarities and differences.
Home Activity: Gather several different rocks and have your child classify them according to characteristics such as hardness, shape, color, smoothness, etc.

Practice Estimating and Measuring

Follow This Procedure

1–5. Record your estimates and measurements in the chart.

Object	Estimate	Actual measurement

Thinking About Your Thinking

Suppose you wanted to estimate and measure the length of your school hallway. Would you use your fingernail and metric ruler as your measuring tools? Why or why not?

_____

_____

_____

_____

Name _____ Date _____

What other measuring tools might be more accurate?

_____

_____

_____

_____

_____

Self-Assessment Checklist	
I **estimated** the length of several objects.	_____
I used a centimeter ruler to accurately measure the length of several objects.	_____
I recorded my estimates and measurements in a chart.	_____
I compared my measurements with my partner's measurements.	_____

Notes for Home Your child estimated the length of several objects.
Home Activity: Choose items in your home and have your child estimate their length and determine which measuring tools should be used to make an accurate measurement.

Practice Inferring

Follow This Procedure

5. Have you ever seen a rainbow? Did it seem similar to what you have just observed?

_____

_____

_____

_____

_____

6. Based on your current observation and past experience, what can you infer about sunlight? Is it made of only one color? Is it a mixture of colors?

_____

_____

_____

_____

_____

_____

Thinking About Your Thinking

List the steps you used to make an inference about the color spectrum of sunlight.

_____

_____

_____

_____

_____

_____

Name _____ Date _____

How did combining past experience with current observations help you draw the correct inference?

_____

_____

_____

_____

_____

_____

Self-Assessment Checklist	
I followed instructions to **observe** the colors made by sunlight reflecting off a mirror.	
I made **inferences** based on my observations.	_____
I listed the steps I used to make an **inference** about the color spectrum of sunlight.	_____

Notes for Home Your child made inferences about the color spectrum of sunlight.
Home Activity: Help your child make an inference about the role of rain in the appearance of a rainbow.

Practice Making Operational Definitions

Follow This Procedure

2. Use the space below to draw an object that produces sound and diagram how the sound is produced.

3. Write an operational definition for the object. What does it do?

_____

_____

_____

_____

_____

_____

Name _____ Date _____

Thinking About Your Thinking

Choose another object and repeat the activity. Compare and contrast the two sound-producing objects. How are they alike and different?

_____

_____

_____

_____

_____

_____

_____

Self-Assessment Checklist	
I drew pictures of two sound-producing objects and diagrammed how the sound is produced from each.	_____
I wrote an **operational definition** for each of the objects.	_____
I compared and contrasted the two sound-producing objects.	_____

Notes for Home Your child wrote an operational definition of a sound-producing object.
Home Activity: Have your child explain the four basic steps in writing an operational definition.

Practice Making and Using Models

Process Skill Activity

Use with page 21.

Follow This Procedure

3–4. Record your observations in the chart.

	Description of what happens to the dots
Blowing the balloon up	
Letting the air out	

5. If this model shows how air particles move as air is heated and cooled, what do the dots represent?

_____

_____

_____

_____

6. What does the process of blowing up the balloon represent?

_____

_____

_____

_____

7. What does the process of letting the air out of the balloon represent?

_____

_____

_____

_____

_____

_____

Thinking About Your Thinking

Explain how this balloon model acts like the particles in air being heated and cooled. Does air expand when it is heated or when it is cooled?

_____

_____

_____

_____

Self-Assessment Checklist	
I **made a model** of how air particles move as air is heated and cooled.	_____
I recorded my **observations** of my model in action in a chart.	_____
I answered questions about what the different parts of my model represent.	_____

 Notes for Home Your child made a model showing how air particles move as air is heated and cooled. **Home Activity:** Help your child think of other situations where a model would be a useful tool for studying something.

Name _____ Date _____

Practice Formulating Questions and Hypotheses

Use with page 23.

Process Skill
Activity

Follow This Procedure

2–3. Record your estimations in the chart.

Object Name	Drop Time	Properties

4. Write a hypothesis about the objects and their drop time.

_____

_____

_____

_____

7. Which properties contributed to a fast drop time?

_____

_____

_____

_____

_____

_____

Thinking About Your Thinking

Was your hypothesis correct? Why or why not?

_____

_____

_____

_____

Self-Assessment Checklist	
I **estimated** the longest to shortest drop times for six different objects.	_____
I wrote a **hypothesis** about the objects and their drop time.	_____
I conducted an **experiment** to test my hypothesis.	_____
I drew **conclusions** about which properties contributed to a fast drop time.	_____

Notes for Home Your child wrote a hypothesis about the drop times of different objects through a cylinder of water.

Home Activity: Have your child explain to you why it is important to the scientific process to formulate questions and hypotheses.

Name _____ Date _____

Practice Collecting and Interpreting Data

Follow This Procedure

2. Record your data in the chart.

	Hours indoors	Hours outdoors
Monday		
Tuesday		
Wednesday		
Thursday		
Friday		
Saturday		
Sunday		
Total		

3. Take the data from your table and reorganize it into a chart or graph. Use different colors for indoor and outdoor time.

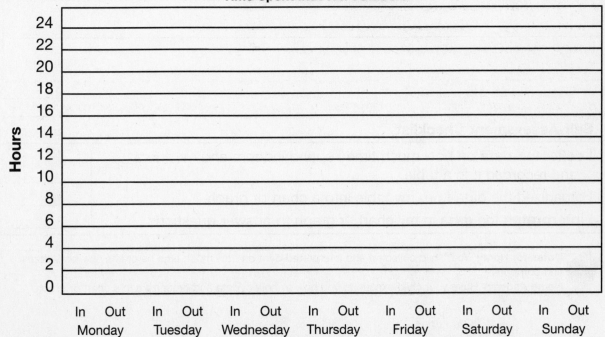

Time Spent Indoors/Outdoors

Name _____ Date _____

4. Interpret the data in your chart or graph to answer the following questions:
Where do you spend the most amount of time, indoors or outdoors?

_____

_____

Do you and your classmates spend the same amount of time indoors during weekdays and weekends?

_____

_____

Can you interpret how you usually spend your "Tuesdays" from just one day of data?

_____

_____

Thinking About Your Thinking

Could you have made as accurate an interpretation of your data if you had only collected data for one day?

_____

Would your data and interpretations vary if you collected it in the summer or the winter? on a holiday?

_____

How can you adjust your data to account for these changes?

_____

_____

Self-Assessment Checklist

I **collected data** on how much time I spend indoors and outdoors and recorded it in a table.	_____
I organized the data from my table into a chart or graph.	_____
I **interpreted** the **data** in my chart or graph to answer questions.	_____

 Notes for Home Your child collected and interpreted data on how much time he or she spends indoors and outdoors.
Home Activity: Have your child explain to you how to collect data and organize it in a chart or graph.

Name _____ Date _____

Practice Identifying and Controlling Variables

Process Skill Activity

Use with page 27.

Follow This Procedure

3–4. Record your data in the chart.

Amount of salt	Length of time for salt to dissolve
1 teaspoon	
2 teaspoons	
3 teaspoons	
4 teaspoons	
5 teaspoons	

Thinking About Your Thinking

Which variable did you change?

_____

_____

_____

_____

What is being tested? (Hint: What did you time?)

_____

_____

_____

_____

Name _____ Date _____

Which variables were kept constant?

_____

_____

_____

What did you find out about how the amount of salt affects the length of time it takes the salt to dissolve?

_____

_____

_____

_____

Self-Assessment Checklist	
I conducted an **investigation** to see how **controlling** one **variable** affects another variable.	_____
I recorded my measurements in a chart.	_____
I determined which variables were changed, which were kept constant, and which responded to the change.	_____

 Notes for Home Your child conducted an experiment to practice controlling and identifying variables.
Home Activity: Have your child explain to you what it means to control variables in an experiment.

Practice Experimenting

Follow This Procedure

2. Write a hypothesis to state which rubber band you think will stretch the most when 500 grams of weight are added.

_____

_____

4. Record the results of your experiment in the chart.

Rubber band width	Length before weight	Length after weight	Difference

6. Graph the results listed in your chart.

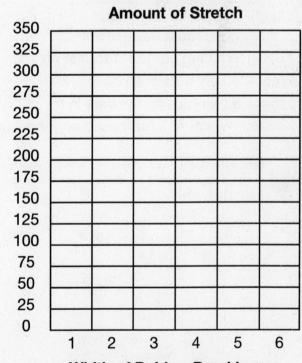

Rubber Band Width and Amount of Stretch

Stretch in millimeters

350
325
300
275
250
225
200
175
150
125
100
75
50
25
0

1   2   3   4   5   6

Width of Rubber Band in mm

Name _____ Date _____

7. State your conclusion.

_____

_____

_____

Thinking About Your Thinking

What did you learn from this investigation? How can having a too-specific hypothesis in the experimental process cause a problem? Can too broad a focus in later steps cause a problem as well? Explain.

_____

_____

_____

_____

_____

_____

Self-Assessment Checklist	
I wrote a **hypothesis** to state which of the rubber bands would stretch the most.	_____
I designed an **experiment** to test my hypothesis.	_____
I recorded my data in a chart.	_____
I made a graph using the data in my chart.	_____
I stated my **conclusion** based on the results of the experiment.	_____

Notes for Home Your child wrote a hypothesis and designed an experiment to test it.
Home Activity: Help your student design an experiment to determine the affects of salt water on fresh water plant growth.